SIX O

al

CORK

Tom McElligott was born in Cork of Kerry parents. A champion handballer in his youth, he has worked as a teacher and educationist in many parts of Ireland and abroad. He now lives with his wife in Sutton, County Dublin, and is a keen gardener. His books include *The Story of Handball* published by Wolfhound Press, *Secondary Education in Ireland 1870-1921* (IAP, 1981), Education in Ireland (IPA, 1966), *This Teaching Life* (Lilliput Press, 1987), and he was editor of the journal *The European Teacher* for fifteen years.

SIX O'CLOCK
all over
CORK

Tom McElligott

WOLFHOUND PRESS

First published 1992 by
WOLFHOUND PRESS
68 Mountjoy Square,
Dublin 1

Wolfhound Press receives financial assistance from the Arts Council/An Chomhairle Ealaíon, Dublin, Ireland.

British Library Cataloguing in Publication Data
A catalogue record for this book is available from the British Library.

ISBN 0-86327-371-8

Acknowledgements
To acknowledge help in compiling a sketch of one's life is to recognise and appreciate the value of friendship. I have leaned heavily, as indeed have so many others, on the help of Seán Beecher, and of Walter McGrath and Steve Coughlan of the *Cork Examiner*. And if on all my visits to Cork I saw a lot of them, I rarely failed to see and make an almost equal demand on Kieran Burke of the Cork City Library and Patricia McCarthy of the Archives Institute.

Táim go mór faoi chomaoin ag Séamus Ó Coigligh, iar-dalta Glaisín, agus Conchubhair Ó Loingsigh (Árd-Mháistir Scoil Náisiúnta an Ghlaisín). A long-standing friendship with C.J.F. MacCarthy ensured his much-valued help and I was never in doubt that Richard Henchion would provide some unusual items of information on Cork and its inhabitants which he generously shared with me. I feel indebted to Ann O'Leary of Messrs Henry Ford & Son Ltd, who made available photographs from the firm's archives.

And if Cork rallied to my calls for help, so too I must admit, did Dublin. Liz Fleeton (TCD), Jim Lynch (National Library), Dallas Camier, Maurice Harmon, Séamas Ó Buachalla and Neil Kennedy sustained me in different ways with advice and information.

Finally, it was Benvenuto Cellini who, though not born in Cork, has some very sapient observations to make on life and on humanity in general. To him is attributed the statement that a wife is sent by heaven to inspire man. And so my thanks for encouragement and inspiration to my wife, Concepta.

Cover photograph: Sean Beecher
Cover design: Jan de Fouw
Typesetting: Wolfhound Press
Printed in the Republic of Ireland by Colour Books, Dublin.

A Town near Blarney

I can never recall a time when I wasn't aware of a pride in claiming Cork as my birthplace. It is rather like being able to trace your ancestry to Adam and Eve or belonging to the Exclusive Brethren. It creates a feeling of confidence and this, in turn, fosters the conviction that the best things in life are to be found there — authors and actors, poets and politicians, hurlers and footballers.

This confidence must at times irritate, the boastfulness infuriate, but it all stems from the irrepressible high spirits, a compound of gaiety and gasconade with which they face life. One never meets renegade Corkonians. All are totally loyal, forever committed to the simple proposition that Cork is the best place in the world. The sound of 'The Banks of my own Lovely Lee' on the evening of an All-Ireland hurling final is enough to banish doubt and recall to their allegiance any strays.

What has made Cork such a close-knit, intensely assertive community is that because of its size one never runs the risk of feeling lost. Everyone seems to know everyone else and each seems equally convinced of the splendour of his birthplace. So it is that when a Corkman goes to live outside the County bounds, he clings tenaciously to the memories of place. This sense of place is linked to a sense of the past and he identifies himself easily with the triumphs and glories of other days.

I was not at all surprised when as a small boy I saw in a baker's window the World Championship Cup for bread-making. It was what I expected. And when later I read in Ripley's column in the *Sunday Express* 'Believe it or Not' that a Corkman, Jerome Collins, had the longest funeral in the world, from the Arctic Circle to Curraghkippane cemetery on the outskirts of Cork city, it was no more than I expected. Much later, as I listened to my mother call out 'Six o'clock all over Cork', my belief that Cork was the centre of the universe was further strengthened.

Tartarin of Tarascon would have felt at home in Cork. It has always had sons to boast of the splendour of Shandon and carry tales of the glories of Patrick Street to the furthest ends of the earth. Nor has it shown much regard for such virtues as modesty and humility when the exploits of its sons are in question. As if in evidence of this, I found myself on one occasion beside a man in a bar on the Douglas Road. His first words to me, a complete stranger, were 'He's the greatest man in the world.' I nodded assent, feeling that nothing else was demanded of me. 'He's out on his own,' he continued, looking somewhat disappointed at my lack of enthusiasm. He then pointed to a short paragraph in the *Cork Examiner* which detailed the achievement of a Corkman, Mick Meaney, who had broken the world record by remaining underground for sixty-one days.

The truth is that modesty does not suit Cork people. There is a certain swagger in their walk, locally known as a *gaatch*, a certain bravado in their speech which even in times of adversity never quite deserts them. I relish the oddities that show in their vocabulary and positively rejoice when I hear the suffix 'ah' which the Cork idiom tends to add to certain words so that Patrick Street becomes *Panah*, Barrack Street *Barrackah*, Farranferris *Farranah*.

Nor are such oddities confined to speech. It comes as no great shock to see that the clock on Shandon steeple differs not infrequently from what is accepted as standard time, that Daunt's Square has but two sides and that the river Lee complicates life for visitors by dividing itself in two as it enters the city. Thus they find themselves crossing bridges only to meet with more bridges spanning what is clearly a different river but which bears the same name. To mystify them even more, the streets appear to curve and twist in an altogether aimless manner, following as they do the underground streams and channels. Small wonder that the Wide Street Commissioners, who in the eighteenth century did so much for Dublin, were reluctant to extend their efforts to Cork.

You can enter the city from many sides but there is nothing to equal the dramatic entry by train. Soon after the train passes Kilbarry and just as Shandon and the cathedral spires come into view, the tunnel cuts off the light and with a great swoosh the train thunders into the Glanmire Station.

It rejoices in the title of 'the Rebel City' though a close examination of its history may leave some doubts as to the accuracy of the label. Since 1900 it has boasted a Lord Mayor, a distinction bestowed on it by Queen Victoria and which it shares with two other Irish cities, Belfast and Dublin. Even in the Cork of my own youth, the word 'royal' still preceded such well-known establishments as The Oyster Tavern and the Victoria Hotel.

A certain perverse instinct seems to have led the citizens to support the losing royalist cause on more than one occasion. They came out in support of Perkin Warbeck when he laid claim to the throne of England in 1497, when the mayor of the city, John Walters, was executed for espousing what was realised too late to be the wrong cause.

Two centuries later, the citizens blundered again when they rallied to the Jacobite standard in support of James I. On that occasion the great fortress known as Elizabeth Fort was commanded by Colonel Roger McElligott who was forced to surrender to the Duke of Marlborough. A euphemism which must be unequalled in the history of modern warfare is to be found in John Windele's *History of Cork* when describing the siege. He writes that 'during Marlborough's siege of Cork its garrison was dreadfully annoyed (presumably by shelling) from the tower of the Cathedral.'

It may be that rebellion against authority always smoulders in a people naturally impetuous and needs only a personality to kindle it into flame. Parnell, it will be remembered, made many of his most inflammatory speeches from the balcony of the old Victoria Hotel in Patrick Street. And who but a Corkman born into a Protestant Unionist family would have kept the Abbey Theatre open as did Lennox Robinson, on the day of King Edward VII's death when all else in Dublin was closed down.

Conflicting loyalties surfaced again when during the First World War the Cork Corporation removed the name of the great Celtic scholar, German-born Kuno Meyer, from the Roll of Freemen of the city.[1] When J.J. Walsh, who was then a postal official in Bradford and later to become Postmaster-General in the Free State Government, wrote protesting against this decision,

---

1. Removed in 1915, restored in 1920.

disciplinary action was taken and he was dismissed.

Yet nowhere did the flame of rebellion burn more brightly than throughout Cork city and county in the years that followed the Rising of 1916. The bitter political rivalries which had divided the citizens during the elections of 1910 into 'O'Brienites', followers of William O'Brien, and 'Molly Maguires', followers of John Redmond, were muted during those years only to surface again after the Treaty. Even then, the divisions which locked Free Staters and Republicans in conflict failed to weaken the ties which made Cork a city of quite unusual communal unity.

This is due in no small measure to its geographical situation. From any of the surrounding hills, whether you approach it from Bandon or Fermoy, from Kinsale or Crosshaven, you find yourself looking down on the amphitheatre that is the old city within which still exists a sort of urbanised clan system. The Telephone Directory lists some thirty columns of subscribers answering to the name Murphy and over twenty columns are devoted to McCarthys.

It was within this amphitheatre that the shadowy figure of the city's patron saint, Finbarr, emerged in the seventh century to found his abbey on the rock of Gilabbey. Around it clustered the first inhabitants and since then their descendants have bestowed the name 'Finbarr' on all manner of institutions, ranging from hospitals to hurling clubs, from a cathedral to a choral society. And it was on the fringe of this, the oldest part of the city, that I was born. On my birth certificate, Daniel Egan, in his capacity as 'Superintendent Registrar of Births, Deaths and Marriages for the district of Cork', recorded my entry into the world as having taken place on 26 August 1914. Under 'Rank or Profession of Father' was entered 'Book-keeper, ex RIC' and my mother's maiden name was given as Rosanna Cadan.

Of my first years I remember little and have often marvelled at the enviable precision with which others record their day-to-day activities during their first months of life. If my birth failed to find mention in the newspapers of the time, there is some evidence of planetary movements which I like to think were not unrelated to my coming. An eclipse of the sun took place on 26 August when 'the light of the sun', according to one report, 'was diminished for some minutes.' The date is also, as is known to all hagiographers, the Feast Day of St Bregwine, archbishop of Canterbury, St Elizabeth Bichier des Ages, St Herluin, St John

Wall, St Mary Desmaisieres, St Pandonia, St Teresa Jornet Ihars and St Zephyrinus, Pope.

How truthful is memory? I have forgotten a great deal but this only serves to make me confident that what I do remember is authentic. I am not, however, relying on memory when I say that on that August day, tea from Bolster's of Patrick Street was two shillings a pound, Midleton 15-year-old liqueur whiskey twenty-five shillings a gallon, and coal twenty-seven shillings a ton from the Cork Steam Packet Company.

For those in need of money to purchase some or all of these items, Farrows Bank in Patrick Street was open on six days of the week. Other services available to the citizens included Grinders (Cutlery) three, Farriers seventeen, Dynamite Agents two, Hatters six, Tanners three and one Oil Skin maker. *Guy's Cork Almanac and Directory*, which supplied all this information, made no attempt to indicate who the customers of the Dynamite Agents or the Oil Skin Maker were likely to have been.

I was baptised in St Finbarr's West, better known as 'the Lough Church'. What added a note of spiritual distinction, or so I always thought, to my baptism was that both my godparents were religious. My godmother was Sister Cecilia Ryan of the Bon Secours Order and my godfather was Rev Arthur McGuinness of the Maynooth Mission to China. The Ryans had a draper's shop on George's Quay and were old friends of my mother while Arthur McGuinness's father had been stationed at Union Quay RIC barracks with my father.

My maternal grandparents had come to Cork in 1886 from Rathmore in county Kerry. They went to live in Wellington Square where most of the houses were then occupied by British Army officers stationed in the city or in Ballincollig. They were impressive-looking, three-storey buildings set around a small park where my mother remembered the uniformed 'nannies' pushing prams along paths beneath the great chestnut trees. Her parents later moved to the city where they had a drapery business at 112 North Main Street.

They saw the coming of the trams and later the appearance on the streets of the first buses and motor-cars. They watched three of their children marry and go to live on the edge of the city — on Highfield Avenue, Ballintemple and Sunday's Well. Fields where they picnicked on Crabapple Lane and Torytop Lane are long lost to the JCB's and concrete-mixers.

My First Home

During my early years I lived with my parents and Margaret, my sister, at Shamrock Lodge on Highfield Avenue which then marked the western end of the city. From my mother's accounts of her own early life, the Cadan household was almost Victorian in the emphasis placed on behaviour, appearance, church-going etc. The children went to school, did their homework, helped in the shop, sang in choirs and had to be indoors by eight o'clock, except on the rare occasions when they went to concerts. She saw to it that our lives were far less regimented and my memory is of a very happy and carefree childhood.

Her father came to live with us after the death of his wife in 1920. He answered to my admittedly vague ideas of what a grandfather should be like. He had a cluster of white curls around his otherwise bald, shiny head. He wore a silver pocket watch and chain which I was permitted to play with while I sat on his knee. He took snuff which made me sneeze and he snored loudly when he fell asleep in his armchair after dinner each day.

My earliest memory of sound is of my mother singing as she went about her housework. She had a wide range of songs drawn from opera and also from appearances on concert platforms with her sisters. Years later I came across mention of 'choral items by the Misses Cadan' in a programme for the Cork Exhibition of 1902. My mother had also taken piano lessons from Tilly Fleischmann who, when her husband was interned as an enemy alien during the First World War, took his place at the organ in the North Cathedral.

My mother was almost fifteen years younger than my father and was ever ready to take part in childish sports while he remained largely an onlooker. I may have been her favourite as my sister was most certainly my father's. She clung tenaciously to the patterns and values established over the years while living with her parents and had become a member of the Third Order of St Francis before her marriage. She used to bring me with her to what I always thought of as a rather odd form of religious observance — the Portiuncula. On the first and second day of August we would visit the Church of St Francis in Liberty Street and say certain prayers inside the church. We would then go out only to return almost at once and repeat the same prayers.

The old church, always referred to as 'Broad Lane', and the flagged yard beside it did look neglected but it was much loved by the people of the Marsh. The massive brick-faced basilica which has replaced it seems almost too ostentatious in that humble setting. My mother made valiant efforts to learn sufficient Irish to be able to respond in church when a priest chose to say the Rosary in Irish but she remained totally out of sympathy with such movements as the Gaelic League, the GAA and what she used disparagingly refer to as 'those fellows in coarse green tweeds'. I think that she was both relieved and happy when, instead of becoming a Fianna boy scout as I might have, I became an altar-boy and later joined the choir of St Peter and Paul's. Each in its own way represented in her eyes a stepping-stone towards salvation.

In childhood a mother means most and with my father out at work for most of the day, I spent much of my time in the kitchen and, when summer came, in the small front garden. Gradually, I became more adventurous. The joy of exploring the immediate neighbourhood even if that never extended beyond a few gardens was one of the delights of childhood. With Bobby McClement from the other side of the avenue, I sailed paper boats on roadside rivulets after heavy rain, rolled marbles on the footpath and, in autumn, played 'conkers' with chestnuts.

As children we all engaged in mock battles with stones. Long before Mr MacAdam discovered his formula for road-making, the limestone quarries around Cork provided an abundance of 'ammunition'. The 'Rules' for such battles obliged all participants to aim only at the feet.

Highfield Avenue runs from the Magazine Road to the College Road and a parallel avenue was called Highfield West. Beyond this was a big house, well hidden in the trees, owned by Dr Joe Giusani who drove one of the first motor-cars in Cork. A sloping field led down to what is today St Clare's Avenue. The suburbs had even then begun to gnaw their way deep into what we called Donovan's Field, where I can recall a sports meeting being held at some time in the early twenties.

My bedroom faced east towards Horgan's Buildings from which we were separated by a lane called Barry's Walk and a field owned by Julia Scraggs where on summer evenings corncrakes held choral festivals. Far from murdering sleep as so many people seem to think, I remember their cries as soothing and companionable. In the morning when the sun lit up the room, I would pull the blind and then rush downstairs to see if my *thorneens* were still alive in a jampot of water and if the apple-seeds I had sown the previous day had grown into trees.

I don't seem to have been photographed as a baby and the earliest photo, carefully preserved in the family archives, shows me astride a rocking-horse wearing a petticoat. The shame of this must have scarcely worn off when I was photographed looking smug and smarmy in a bottle-green velvet suit and wearing a cossack-style fur hat. Later still and much my favourite is a photo taken when I was about four. It shows me àgainst an improbable background of palms, wearing a brass-buttoned navy coat and a sailor hat marked 'HMS Victory'.

A framed photograph of a police tug-o-war team dated 1891, with my father prominent in the front row, hung in the kitchen. In the sitting-room (the word 'drawing-room' had no meaning for me) a carefully-posed photo of my father and mother on their wedding-day stood on the piano. Neither of them is smiling: in 1910 marriage vows were not taken lightly.

I was always happy in my own company and would spend hours blowing bubbles with clay pipes in the scullery and playing imaginary games of hurling in a back yard no bigger than a large room, using the kitchen door as one goal and a gate leading to the garden as the other.

The National School

I was enrolled in the class of 'Mixed Infants' at Glasheen School in the autumn of 1918. When the school was opened in 1897 it consisted of two classrooms for boys with an adjoining two-roomed school for girls. Additional classrooms were added later. The village of Glasheen had once been the site of a cotton factory and the bleaching green lay just across the road from the school. This was the Sadlier Mill where at the height of its activity fifty people were employed and over three hundred weavers worked from their homes between Factory Hill and Wilton.

When I started going to school, Glasheen consisted of a dozen small houses, a shop owned by Katie Kelleher and one public house, Flannery's. Liquorice all-sorts, lucky dips, barley sugar, Cleeve's toffee and bull's eyes were her stock in trade. Boiled sweets were kept in big glass jars and cigarettes were sold loose as well as in packets. You got two cigarettes for a 'lop' (one penny) and one cigarette for a 'make' (halfpenny). To us it was the most wonderful shop in the world. Woolworth's in Patrick Street was bigger but there you would not get four sherbet dabs for a penny.

Overlooking the village is Sheares Ville, once the home of John and Henry Sheares, hidden behind masses of apple and chestnut trees. The house, which has been continuously lived in for close on three hundred years, was purchased by their grandfather, Humphrey Sheares, in 1703. The business interests of the family were in the city but in the eighteenth century Glasheen was sufficiently far out to afford them the pleasures of country life.

Henry Sheares senior, a merchant banker and an MP, had sent the two boys to Trinity College and it was while studying there that they became members of the United Irishmen. When this became known to the authorities, efforts were made to get them to reveal the names of their associates. To this end, no less a personage than Lord Clare, Chancellor of Ireland, had a meeting with them in the house of another Cork banker, John Roche. When they refused to reveal names to him, he had them arrested and brought for trial to Green Street Courthouse in Dublin.

The trial began on 26 June, 1798 and on 13 July of the same year Lord Carleton pronounced sentence of death. The Attorney-General, John Toler, possibly fearing an attempt to rescue them, asked that 'execution be done upon the prisoners' on the following day. They were both hanged and Henry's body beheaded. They are buried in the crypt of St Michan's Church in Dublin.

My first teacher was Miss Florence Sheridan and my first efforts at forming letters were made on a slate while sitting beside a stove with a metal mesh safeguard. We learnt to count with the aid of coloured beads on a ballframe.

When we graduated to Senior Infants, we were introduced to the joys of filling inkwells from earthenware jars, in which we mixed ink powder and water, and were taught to use dip pens with 'J' nibs and 'N' nibs. That advance led us to Vere Foster's headline copybooks in which we sought to imitate handwriting which seemed to be no better than that of our teacher, Mr Fehily. I can still recall some of the copperplate headlines: 'Apply thine heart unto instruction', 'Be not weary in well doing', 'Commit thy Way unto the Lord's'. All very improving but with little meaning for six-year-olds.

We recited our lessons aloud and with the aid of a small table-book learned to add, subtract and multiply but only, I think, up to the number twelve. It appeared that no one could possibly want the answer to any number greater than twelve multiplied by twelve. Sums of even the simplest kind I could not do. Much later, other and no less able teachers were to discover that no method had been devised which would enable them to teach me anything of Algebra or Geometry. Yet, oddly enough, stray wisps of knowledge remain with me so that I am able to inform anyone anxious to know that there are two thousand, two hundred and forty lb in a ton and that a 'weight' is a measure of twenty-one lb — but I am never asked.

Many years after leaving school, I walked along the school path to the Glasheen Road end. There, leaning on the swing-gate, I listened to an unchanging chant: 'Twelve inches one foot, three feet one yard, five and a half yards one perch, forty perches one furlong, eight furlongs one mile'. Unchanging and unquestioning, until 1972 came along to shift an age-old allegiance and propel our children into the metric age.

We also recited in unison both the questions and answers in Butler's Catechism as used in the diocese of Cork. Even to this day, given the question, I can usually provide the answer. For example, in the unlikely event of my being asked, 'What is forbidden by the Sixth Commandment?' I can at once reply, 'All immodest actions, looks and words, all immodest songs, novels and plays, and everything that is contrary to chastity.' As for stories of Adam and Eve, their behaviour in the Garden of Eden was entirely secondary to the excitement we felt when, in an illustration in Schuster's *Bible Stories*, we saw the serpent watching them with blazing eyes.

Sullivan's *Geography* ensured that we knew the height of the world's highest mountain, the length of the longest river, and the depth of the deepest ocean as well as the principal towns of every county in Ireland together with capes, rivers, ports, etc.

On Saturday when the school was closed, my mother sent myself and my sister to confession. This she did on every Saturday of the year whether or not we had committed any breaches of the Ten Commandments. It left my mother free to put black-lead on the range, Brasso on the stair-rods, Mansion polish on the floor, while in the church we chattered and twittered and darted from one confessional box to another.

It was also a day for borrowing books from the Children's Library in the Father O'Leary Hall on the Bandon Road. Mother had read stories to us from an early age and I recall the pleasure of listening to *Children of the New Forest*, *Martin Rattler*, *Red Cloud*, and *Grimm's Fairy Tales* as we sat by the kitchen fire on winter afternoons. We were not encouraged to read comics but the embargo did not extend to borrowing them. While no one, certainly no boy, would be seen dead reading *Chick's Own*, *Rainbow* was highly thought of because it contained the adventures of Tiger Tim. The *Magnet* and *Gem* were for more 'advanced' readers and not until we were almost leaving the National School did we turn to Sexton Blake.

School introduced me to *Séadna* which, besides being an exciting story for young people, gives one a grasp of spoken Irish thanks to the talkativeness of Nora an Tochair, Bab a Leasa and their companions. Irish was well taught throughout the school and An tAthair Peadar Ó Laoghaire's use of the language to translate such stories as *Aesop's Fables* provided an excellent base for later study. As we moved up through the school we were passed on to different teachers, two of whom, Sean Ó Briain and Jack Crowley, were native speakers. Even those who showed least enthusiasm could speak a fair amount of Irish by the time they finished in 6th Class and this was achieved with little or no corporal punishment.

As in all the old National Schools the windows at Glasheen were set high, affording no more than a glimpse of the sky. The teacher's chair and table were set on a rostrum from which he could watch for the coming of that most feared of all officials, the schools inspector.

On the window-sills might be found jars of frogspawn from the nearby marshland, geranium pots and, in season, clumps of primroses and sprays of fuchsia. Wall decorations were sparse: a rather tattered map of Ireland, a colour chart showing a girl milking a cow, a man shoeing a horse and a man cutting turf. A small board showed the number of pupils in each class on that day.

The dry closet that served close on one hundred boys was partly concealed by nettles and was too evil-smelling to be visited except *in extremis*.

'On the lang' was our phrase for 'mitching'. It was not considered too serious an offence and only when the attendance figure for the whole school showed a tendency to fall was the School Attendance Officer asked to investigate. Absences were almost always due to illness as most pupils called for their friends as they made their way along the road to school.

One of the delights of walking to school was the abundance and variety of life which we encountered on the way. Each morning, clutching my sister's hand, I set off on the walk of over a mile to school. We went through Cooney's market gardens on the Magazine Road past hedges of hawthorn and ash to where the road dipped down to the orchards owned by Youngs, Donovans and Coughlans. That mile of road was rich in plant, bird and animal life.We were on friendly terms with the milkman's horse, the breadvan driver's horse and the ponies that pushed their heads over the hedges to munch the clumps of grass we offered them.

I believe that among the civilizing influences of early life is that of walking to school. I have since read that in Japan walking to school is obligatory and the Japanese government plays its part by providing a primary school within walking distance of every rate-paying dwelling.

We learnt the changes the seasons bring: we bravely walked through silver cobwebs and kicked our way through crisp leaves in autumn, built a snowman in the schoolyard when it snowed and welcomed the first green leaves of the whitethorn, which we ate as 'bread and cheese', in the springtime.

We came to recognise the different milkcarts which came in from Coolowen, Doughcloyne, Chetwynd and from more distant Inniscarra. Milk was delivered 'loose' and to the pint or pints asked for by the housewife, the milkman always added a 'tilly' i.e. an extra sup. He called morning and afternoon and if I answered his knock, I would then bring the jug of milk into the pantry where my mother covered it with a muslin-cloth weighed down with a row of brightly-coloured glass beads.

I liked our milkman, Tim O'Leary of Springmount Dairy in Carrigrohane, because he allowed me to sit up on the seat beside him. I could then watch the plump rump of the horse swaying between the shafts, hold the reins while he stopped to deliver milk and with his help press the wooden brake blocks as we went down the hill to the College Road.

In my eight years at Glasheen School I cannot recall any organised games or school tours. We had no need of them. We went bird- nesting during lunchtime in the nearby St Finbarr's Cemetery, played 'kick-the-can' on the road in front of the school, chased one another through the fields and improvised tug-o-war games with straw ropes. It would in fact be easy to convince me that today's children of national school age are to some extent 'over organised' and that left to themselves they will improvise their own games.

Only once do I remember a hurling match being played which involved the school. That was when a northside team from Trimbath's Lane National School issued a challenge which was accepted. For an event of such importance it was decided that Jim Buttimer, later to keep goal for Cork, should be persuaded to remain at school for a seventh year. He sat on a bench in the Sixth Year classroom but, as befitted a mature scholar of about fourteen, no teacher addressed any questions to him.

The high reputation enjoyed by Glasheen School may have

been due in part to the small turn-over of staff. I can remember but one change in my years there and that was when Mr Clancy retired. Parents related well to teachers by whom they themselves had been taught and the work within the school benefited in continuity. Teachers were expected to assist in organising local social, cultural and recreational events which might or might not include training choirs and ensuring attendance at the Children's Mass on Sundays. There was a harmonium in the girls' school which emitted reasonably pleasant sounds at Christmas and on other occasions when a concert was held in the school.

Out of Doors

On summer days, once school was over, my sister and myself sat in the front garden making daisy-chains or were brought for a walk as far as Cáit Shea's Lane at the end of the Model Farm Road. Small cottages flanked the road, each with its bird-cage for linnet or canary hanging beside the half-door. My mother always stopped at an ivy-covered house to call on Minnie Ahern, an aunt of the Beckett family — hurlers every one of them, father and five sons, with Sarsfields and St Finbarr's. A short path off the main road led to the Munster Institute, better known as 'the Model Farm', where rather superior-looking hens strutted round in neatly-netted, half-acre 'runs'. Printed notices indicated the family names of the residents in each 'run': Light Sussex, Rhode Island Reds, Buff Leghorns, White Wyandottes, Black Minorcas. My mother bought eggs which were packed in a stout cardboard box which I was allowed to carry.

Just opposite the gate of the Model Farm in a recess on the side of the road a stone-breaker sat beside what appeared to be a small mountain of limestone rock. His must have been one of the loneliest jobs in the world — to sit through the day with a piece of sacking over his shoulders and only a pair of wire goggles as protection against rock splinters.

emaciated
goggled manikin
ever chipping at the stones
that filled our roads,
his double hammer
rhythms, jigs, jog
memories:
('Penates', *Carnival*, Seamus Cashman, Monarch Line [Dublin] 1988.)

We were always glad when walks with our mother led towards 'the Lough'. There we could sail toy boats, feed the swans and try to entice roach into a net . On the stretch of ground separating the water from Hartland's Nurseries, donkey and cycle races were held. The prizes, if we are to credit an advertisement of the time, were somewhat different from those offered for similar events today: cards of Blakey's Boot Protectors, gooseberry bushes, and bagpipes!

While we must have heard the story many times, we always insisted that our mother should again tell us the legend of 'the Lough'.

She always began by telling us that beneath the waters lay a city of tall towers and wonderful palaces. Hidden within the city was a treasure which had been stolen from a king who vowed to bestow the hand of his daughter on he who would recover the treasure. The princess had eyes only for a poor but handsome youth who to win her dived down beneath the waters. When he did not return, her father had her betrothed to another but before the wedding-day came, she died of a broken heart.

John Fitzgerald, the Bard of the Lee, recalls the legend in a poem entitled 'The Lost Diver' which ends with the lines,

This is the cause why at summer's eve,
If lovers stray 'round the shore,
Their eyes will moisten, their hearts will grieve,
For the diver that came no more.

'The Lough', too, has its place in history and we are told that James II, after landing at Kinsale, entered the city by Togher Road and that his horses refreshed themselves at the lake waters.

Living on the road leading to the lake was a retired RIC sergeant named Smith who, my mother pointed out to me with pride, was one of those chosen to march with other 'sons of the Empire' in Queen Victoria's Jubilee procession. The *Cork Constitution* of 24 June, 1897, quoted from an English journal on that occasion, 'I believe that we are all agreed that the Royal Irish Constabulary made a brave show, and certainly they attracted unusual attention, for it was rumoured about town that the finest and handsomest members of the RIC were specially picked out for the Diamond Jubilee and that these big sons of the Green Isle were veritable creatures of beauty!'

The Lough parish, which at that time extended no farther than Wellington Square, was neither excessively poor nor excessively rich. A skilled working class lived close to if not side by side with clerical workers, shop owners, teachers, solicitors, corporation and county council employees. There never was anything like the same concentration of industry on the south side as on the north side of the city. Old-established firms like Goulding's, Denny's and Murphy's Brewery as well as the more recent Sunbeam and Harringtons were all located in the Blackpool area. Beamish and Crawford's Brewery and the Lee Boot Factory were the chief employers of labour south of the North Gate Bridge.

Side by side with the comfortable middle-class residents, on the avenues leading off the Magazine and College Roads, were poorer areas on the streets and lanes leading down towards the city centre. I have, however, always felt that poverty may have been less hard to bear in a city where living standards were not dramatically different and where there was little or no 'luxury living' at the top.

Apart from the Ford factory, most of the industries providing employment were relatively small concerns and therefore unlikely to cause widespread distress when forced to lay off workers. At the same time I can recall small groups gathered outside the pawnshops on Barrack Street on a Monday morning waiting for them to open, a scene no different from that described by Walter Greenwood in *Love on the Dole* where he recounts how the family clothes were given to Mr Price, the pawnbroker, on Monday to be redeemed on Friday.

The Troubled Years

I was too young to recall the years of the First World War though I do have a memory of seeing a big sack of flour standing inside the kitchen door. Doubtless, white flour was in short supply at the time and my father may have got it from Sutton's where he was then working.

I was much more aware of the inconveniences, to use no stronger a word, imposed on the people when the Black and Tans and the Auxiliaries attempted to assert the authority of the British Crown. Movements were restricted after lighting-up time and while my parents had a pass which entitled them to use the Gaol Walk which led from the Gaol Cross to the avenue where we lived, we were still challenged by a sentry at the point where today a footbridge spans the road and leads from one building in the university to another.

While police patrols were being ambushed daily, my father cannot have felt that he, a former member of the RIC, was in any danger and I was with him more than once when he called to see his old comrades at the police headquarters on Union Quay. He also continued to frequent the Queen's Hotel in Parnell Place which was owned by an ex-RIC sergeant named Ryan and which was regarded as the unofficial 'mess' of the force in Cork.

From those who knew him, I gather that he was almost excessively law-abiding and he cannot have found it easy to live through the years when the Black and Tans and Auxiliaries were the agents of law and order in the country.

He had at one time to face the moral dilemma which confronted so many Irish families. Should he or should he not shelter a blood relative, Jack McElligott, who, while studying Engineering at UCC, was 'on the run'? To do so at a time when houses were being raided daily was to take a considerable risk.

Inside the front door of every house a list of those residing there had to be displayed and anyone whose name did not appear on the list and who was found there was liable to arrest. He did shelter him but I wonder what discussions he had with my mother before doing so.

A clerk who worked with him at Sutton's, where he was employed after his retirement, told me of my father's high regard for W.T. Cosgrave and with what satisfaction he had bought shares in the First National Loan. I am happy at the thought that before his death he enjoyed a few years of peace during which a native government restored a measure of security at least to part of the country.

During the troubled times Cork was heavily policed. Few of the barracks held more than three or four policemen whose chief duties were to become familiar with the neighbourhood and to watch for signs of 'riot, commotion and civil strife'. Units of the IRA systematically destroyed many of the suburban barracks and I can recall seeing burning barracks on the College Road, at Dennehy's Cross and at Victoria Cross, all within an area of one square mile. Apart from the barracks at Union Quay, Cat Fort and King Street (now MacCurtain Street), most of them were scarcely distinguishable from other buildings except for the harp surmounted by a crown over the door.

The British Army sentries on duty outside the City Jail often asked me to do messages for them at a nearby shop, O'Riordan's on the College Road. Whether getting a packet of Woodbines or a few currant buns could be interpreted as 'giving succour and sustenance to the enemy', I never found out. The reward of a penny was sufficient to ensure my services if not my loyalty.

As young children, our out-of-door activities were seriously curtailed by curfew restrictions imposed by the military authorities during the years 1920-21. This meant that everyone had to be indoors by the time, — sometimes as early as 4 pm — that the patrols left Victoria Barracks.

One of those who dared the patrols on at least one occasion was Mary Bowles from Clogheen. She was credited with the capture of a Lewis gun during an ambush at the top of Strawberry Hill which led to a song, the refrain of which was,

Mary Bowles is on the run,
She ran away with a Lewis gun.

My mother was very frightened when one evening a patrol tramped up the avenue to see that the curfew was being observed. My father was smoking a cigarette in the front garden when an officer drew his revolver and rested it on the bars of the gate, at the same time ordering my father to get inside. My father must have been in no hurry to obey the order as the officer repeated the command. Many years later, Rose Aherne who lived across the road told me that she had fainted, so certain was she that my father was about to be shot.

My own clearest memory of those days is of being lifted up by my father to watch the flames rising high above the burning city when on a December night in 1920 the Black and Tans and Auxiliaries, in retaliation for an ambush in which some of their men were killed, set fire to Patrick Street and the City Hall. On the following morning, which was a Sunday, he brought me down town where firemen were still playing hoses on the smouldering ruins. While our house was never raided nor were my parents ever searched, I did see Auxiliaries whipping the jarveys on the South Mall where they had a rank.

Sports fixtures in the city and county were seriously affected during 'the Troubles' not alone because of the action of the authorities in banning matches but also because many players were 'on the run'. Joe Kearney, Jim Hurley, Pádraig Ó Domhnaill, 'Nudge' Callanan and Donal O'Donoghue, all members of the University hurling and football clubs, were on wholetime active service with Tom Barry's Flying Column until the signing of the treaty.

My most vivid memory of the time is of standing on a low wall opposite the University gate on the Western Road to witness the funeral of the Lord Mayor of Cork, Tomás MacCurtain, in March 1920. His only son, a small boy of my own age, wearing the uniform of the Cork Volunteer Pipers Band, walked behind his father's coffin. The Pipe-Major of the band was Neilus Cronin, a gentle, gifted musician whose own funeral I attended ten years later.

I am sometimes asked if I had formed any views on the RIC through knowing my father and meeting his friends. I know that I always resent the implication that in some way they were to be identified with the Black and Tans. Certainly, those ex-RIC men whom I met were contemptuous of the type recruited to form the Black and Tans.

Their own background was so different — many of them, like my father, sons of small farmers. As a force they were respected even when disliked, deeply conservative and known to be especially ambitious for their children.

After the Treaty

J ust as important events which may affect our lives seem often to be linked in our minds with quite ordinary events, so do I associate my parents' joy at the signing of the Treaty with the singing of 'Óró, 'sé do bheatha abhaile' at school. There was a spontaneity, an enthusiasm about this simple song that owed little to words or music. It was the expression of a nation's happiness at the release from English gaols of thousands of political prisoners. Denis Breen, the Cork-born Inspector of Music, conducted the massed choirs of the city's National Schools in singing it at the Opera House in the summer of 1922 and the strains of the melody still echo in my memory.

Óró, 'sé do bheatha abhaile: óró, 'sé do bheatha abhaile
Óró, 'sé do bheatha abhaile anois ar theacht an tsamhraidh.

The day the Treaty was signed is remembered in my family as the day when grandfather 'took a drop too much' to drown his sorrow at what he saw as the end of the Empire he had long served. He had walked as far as Denroche's Cross, a short distance from our house, called to a public house later known as 'Cissie Young's' and emerged in fighting form. Normally the least aggressive of octogenarians, with his pink cheeks, mild blue eyes and white locks, he was seen to attack with his walking-stick a 'gaza' ('gaslamp' to linguistic purists), which had been painted green, white and orange. Then, muttering to himself, he tottered along to the top of the avenue where my mother, ever anxious to avoid a breath of scandal, was waiting to pilot him home.

He was, perhaps, recalling his childhood in county Cavan where, as my mother told us, old soldiers, many of them disabled, came seeking alms at his father's house. They were veterans of

Waterloo who had served under Wellington, after whom 'loyal Cork' named a square and a terrace of houses!

The weeks after the signing of the Treaty were a confusing time for a child of seven. Men with armlets took over the policing of the city pending the formation of the Civic Guards but there were still spasmodic outbreaks of gunfire and midnight arrests.

As children we were familiar, especially in the early part of 1922, with such matters as gaol breaks, hunger-strikes, the sound of armoured cars and the casual round-up of suspects. In imitation of our parents, we became little Republicans and little Free Staters and I can recall having my nose pressed into the mud for espousing the cause of the Free State in words which went something like this:

> Hurray for Michael Collins, he's the champion of our land
> We'll follow him to battle with the orange, green and white,
> And when we get to battle, we'll show de Valera how to fight
> And we'll crown Michael Collins king of Ireland.

Very frightening for a child of eight was the Sunday morning when I saw men get up, genuflect and leave the church in the middle of mass as the priest began reading the joint pastoral of October 1922 condemning the Republican resistance to the Provisional government as 'morally only a system of murder and assassination of the National forces'. It was not unknown for clergymen to receive threatening letters and my father gave a silver-mounted pistol, which he had received as a present from his friend, Captain Francis O'Neill, the Cork-born Chicago police chief, to Father Pat O'Toole of St Finbarr's West.

Geraldine Neeson, art critic and musician, tells of how when she went to confession at the Church of the Holy Trinity and told the priest that as a member of Cumann na mBan she had been excommunicated[1], his reply was that he was only interested in her sins. 'And that,' she adds, 'was all the difference that excommunication meant to me and, apparently, to him.'

Cork was at that time a divided city, how deeply divided it is hard to say. Dillon's Cross, Blarney Street, Barrack Street and Bandon Road were mainly Republican strongholds where the No. 1 Cork Brigade had popular support. When Michael Collins came to Cork to address a meeting in the spring of 1922, he did

1. The Bishop's pronouncement was issued on 13 December 1920.

so because he wanted to rally support for the Treaty. He spoke from a platform beside the National Monument on the Grand Parade, and the crowd, estimated at 50,000, stretched down to the junction of the Grand Parade and Washington Street. It was probably one of the last monster meetings made popular a century earlier by Daniel O'Connell. The date was 12 March 1922 and John O'Sullivan of the *Cork Examiner* has left a record of the occasion as he remembered it: 'Those of an age to remember will recall the extraordinary meeting addressed by Michael Collins on the Grand Parade shortly before the Civil War began with an attack on the Four Courts. For many, including myself, it was the first opportunity to see the great man in the flesh and we did so under circumstances which were unbelievably dramatic. The enormous gathering, possibly the largest ever to assemble at that famous meeting place, was full of enthusiasm for him but mingled with the crowd were scores of young men bent on ensuring that he would not get a hearing. To achieve this they discharged into the air volley after volley of revolver shots which would have created panic in any crowd less accustomed to the sound of firing'.[2]

When the Civil War broke out, the Cork Brigade, which formed part of the Southern Division of the IRA, remained firmly anti-Treaty. Free State troops were sent by sea from Dublin with orders to capture the city but with instructions that they were not to land if they met with any serious resistance. They landed at Passage West in August 1922, two hundred and thirty-two years after Marlborough had landed there on a similar mission.

The Republican resistance was based in Douglas and when the village was taken there was nothing to check the advance on the city. One of those killed during that advance when Free State troops swooped down from the Rochestown Road and the hills above Mount Verdon was a Scot, Ian MacKenzie-Kennedy. He had joined the IRA in 1918 and served in mid-Cork while staying at Tuirín Dubh, the home of Liam and Tadhg Ó Tuama. A tablet to his memory was erected in Douglas.

The retreating Republicans set fire to Victoria Barracks, the Bridewell and Shandon Street Barracks before withdrawing to the west of a line between Macroom and Dunmanway. They commandeered lorries, motor-cars and even jarvey-cars.[3]

My own memory of their flight is of crouching in the garden

2. J. O'Sullivan, *Cork Examiner Jubilee Supplement*, 31 August 1966.

of a neighbour, Mrs Adams, as lorries and Lancia cars swept up the avenue. The men wore trench coats, peak caps (what we called 'spoggers') and carried rifles. It was a sad end to the hopes of many who had fought the Black and Tans and now found themselves divided from their comrades.

One morning in that same summer of 1922 I was awakened by the sound of rushing feet on Barry's Walk[4] which ran behind our house. Twelve Republican prisoners had tunnelled through the wall of the City Gaol opposite the La Retraite Convent. The *Cork Examiner* in reporting the incident said, in what may have been an attempt to explain the failure of the authorities to re-capture them, 'the belief is that none of those who escaped were regarded as of much military importance'.

Commandant Scott, who was then the officer in charge of the Free State forces in the city, was reprimanded but not dismissed. Shortly afterwards he figured in another incident which was to cost a man his life. Scott was visiting Mount Nebo in Blarney Street where Mrs Powell, a sister of Michael Collins, lived with her husband and family. Scott surprised and tackled a raider whom he disarmed. The man, William Healy of Dublin Street, Blackpool, was tried, found guilty of illegal possession of arms and executed at Cork Gaol on 13 March, 1923. Scott later resigned from the army and was ordained priest for the Liverpool diocese.

Gradually, Cork and its citizens accustomed themselves to the appearance of soldiers in green uniform, though occasionally British soldiers and sailors from the harbour forts at Camden and Carlisle were still to be seen in the streets. It was at this critical time in the nation's history that the provisional government took the step of disarming the police. It was a brave decision and it did a great deal to underline the moral authority of an unarmed force. Life on our avenue became more animated as memories of curfew receded. Chalk marks on the pavement indicated that games of hop-scotch, locally known as 'picki', were in progress while wooden tops, marbles, skipping-ropes and hoops again made their seasonal appearance as did knife-grinders, chimney-sweeps and the man offering paper windmills in return for empty jam jars.

3. One of these was driven by Mr Russell who had an undertaker's business at the corner of Green Street and Barrack Street.

4. Also known as Wellington Avenue.

We improvised sporting events such as long jumps, high jumps and sprints in Donovan's Field. Miniature hurling matches (we were mostly under ten) were held on a bare stretch of ground on Highfield West. Teams were selected in a most impartial manner. Each player threw his hurley on the ground, the two captains were chosen and from the pile of hurleys each captain, who was blindfolded, in turn picked a hurley. In that way two teams were chosen.

Possibly because the revived Olympic Games were being held in that year but more probably because I had long legs, my name was entered for the Children's Race at the Drapers Sports of 1924. Now the Drapers Sports was the biggest event of the sporting calendar in Cork and for the Children's Race the prizes were positively mouth-watering! A jam-dish, a coloured pencil, and a paint-box were the awards for the first three to the tape.

I presented myself for my heat bare-footed, as did almost all the other competitors, with braces (by O'Gorman's of Castle Street) and buttons tested to ensure that they would take the strain of my efforts. A shot rang out and we were off. I ended last in a field of eight and decently enough the judges waited until I had finished. Then a kindly man wearing an official badge took my arm and said, ever so gently, 'We won't be needing you again, sonny.'

That ended any ideas I may have had of breaking land speed records and though I was even less successful in water, I did achieve a certain distinction in that element.

It happened this way. A few of us used go to the Corporation Baths in Eglinton Street where with the help of two others, one on either side, I used to manage to dog-paddle my way the breadth of the baths. At that time the *Daily Sketch* featured a Youth Club column which had as its aim the encouragement of initiative and courage among young people. Some of my friends had the bright idea of submitting my name for the club's Medal of Honour which was awarded for some unusual feat of daring. In proposing my name, they wrote explaining that I had, at risk of my life, dived into the river Lee in flood and saved one or it may have been several lives.

Knowing nothing of this, I was surprised to receive a small packet bearing an English stamp. Unaccustomed to getting mail, I opened it with some care. It contained a gilt medal inscribed 'For Valour' and a printed citation outlining what I had supposedly done. What made me tremble was that the accompanying letter expressed the hope that it might be possible to have the Lord Mayor make the formal presentation. I hurriedly wrote a letter of thanks and expressed regret that anything in the nature of a formal presentation would not be possible as I was leaving that day for the US.

Some thirty years passed by before I again found myself taking part in what was mistakenly described as a sporting event. This was at a school sports in Dublin where the Parents' Race attracted an aggressive collection of fathers, each determined to win the prize — an anaemic-looking bottle of wine. This time I fell and in falling brought down my nearest competitor who turned upon me quite savagely.

It may be that school sports need a sponsor or sponsors so that parents will in future line up at the tape resplendent in t-shirts bearing the name, I would suggest, of some local TD or County Councillor. This in turn would lead to the grading and eventually the seeding of competitors, thus ensuring that any aged parents like myself will, should they fall, be at once put down!

Going into Town

After my sister went to boarding school in Carrickmacross, I often accompanied my mother when she went shopping. Such excursions followed an unchanging pattern. Levis's in Castle Street for general groceries where Jimmy Levis or one of the assistants would be sure to invite me to choose a biscuit from the glass-fronted biscuit tins in front of the counter, then to Griffins in the English Market for meat and from his stall to that of Miss Hurley for butter — Black Swan or Queen of the West.

Fish we ate only on Fridays and then my mother went either to Russell's in Princes Street or the Baltimore Stores in MacCurtain Street. Bread could be bought in a variety of shops and in a variety of shapes. In the North Main Street alone there were half a dozen different bakers — D'Arcy, Curran, Simcox, Hosford, O'Shea and at the Castle Street corner, Larry McCarthy. The shapes that bread came in depended very much on the shop but most offered pans, ducks, baskets, castles, cottage loaves and plain loaves.

Shopping in the large drapery stores was more exciting than elsewhere. Overhead wires were used to deal with cash transactions and almost all transactions were cash. An assistant took the money, wrapped it with the docket and put it in a small canister. Then something like a catapult sent the canister flying across the wires until it reached the cashier. Receipt and change, if any, came hurtling back with a speed that would make credit-card users envious. There was one of these at each counter in Dwyer's of Washington Street, a firm which must have clothed most of the population not alone of the city but of the county.

Altogether more enthralling than food shops or drapery stores was the 'Penny Bazaar' in Patrick Street where a great array of trays held, at least for a child's eyes, the treasures of Aladdin's

Cave. It was dimly lit, which served to make a visit even more thrilling. The items on display resembled the contents of a Christmas stocking — mouth organs, paint boxes, flash-lamps, rainbow-transfers, jigsaw puzzles, snakes and ladders, clay bubble pipes.

Next to the bazaar was Hymie Nathan's tailoring establishment. His business methods were unusual; he took the order on one side of Patrick Street, but all measurements and fittings took place on the other side. When I first met him, I asked if he could make a suit for me. His somewhat unexpected reply was 'I could make a suit for a gooseberry.' While I have no reason to believe that the accuracy of the statement was ever tested, I believe he could. He was first-class.

There were a number of shops whose owners had always been closely identified with the national movement — Wallace's in St Augustine Street, Peg Duggan's in Oliver Plunkett Street, O'Mahony's on Washington Street and, of course, Liam Russell's bookshop. To none of these was my mother at all likely to give her custom; their views simply were not hers. She did however bring me in to buy some of my schoolbooks from Liam Russell, whom she had known since the days when he was serving his time with her cousin, Con O'Keeffe, in what was then Old George's Street.

If at the end of an afternoon spent shopping I had not too noticeably shown my impatience, my mother might yield to my entreaties to be allowed watch a horse being shod. There was then almost in the centre of the city a forge owned by 'Pa' McGrath, a one-time Lord Mayor of Cork. I delighted in watching the bellows blow the fire to flame, sending sparks like fireworks up to the dark roof while all the time a horse stood quietly by.

No shopping was ever done on a Sunday simply because so very few shops opened. Almost everyone worshipped and the religious divide in the community showed clearly in the choice of church. Catholics came up the avenue and attended mass at St Finbarr's West, while Protestants went down the avenue to worship in St Fin Barre's Cathedral. Mass-going was a formal affair for which families dressed with particular care. I can remember my sister wearing elastic button-boots, my mother in a suit with fur tippet and muff and my father very elegant and, weather permitting, wearing patent-leather shoes and spats.

The Latin mass remains for me a totally different ceremony

from that which has replaced it. The congregation may not have understood the words but there was what there is not today, a sense of the mystery of the sacrifice. From the opening words of the priest, 'Introibo ad altare Dei', they were, even if it was but for one half-hour, in a world removed from that of their daily lives. And at the end they murmured with sincerity the words that caused me to tremble, 'thrust Satan down to hell and with him all the other wicked spirits who wander through the world for the ruin of souls'.

Games on the road were not favoured on Sundays but on all other days we played until Thompson, the lamplighter, came up the avenue to light the gaslamps and we were then called in to do homework. Each evening when he had read the *Evening Echo*, my father polished all the shoes and repaired those in need of repair, putting protectors on the toecaps and *taoibhíní* on the sides where the leather had given way. He might then take down his violin and play simple dance tunes he had learned in his youth while my mother patched our clothes and darned socks.

Parental restrictions, entirely incomprehensible to children, decided who was to play with whom on the avenue. We never really played in one another's houses and I can remember only one house, McClement's, to which my sister and I were invited. Nor did we welcome 'outsiders' from such parts of the parish as Gilabbey Street and Croaghtamore. Indeed, had a moat and drawbridge sealed off the avenue from nearby settlements such as Horgan's Buildings and Hibernian Buildings, it could not have more effectively sheltered us from contact with them than did our own taboo.

Children can be extraordinarily exclusive in their choice of friends and while we did share our games with those of our own age from Highfield West, it was only just. We retreated within the stockade afforded by our gates and gardens whenever strange children appeared and no visitation from the Goths and Huns of an earlier age could have been more feared than that of gangs of children from 'Spud Town'. This was the name given to an ill defined area reached through an archway beside Denroche's Cross. Their depredations were not of a serious nature; they threw stones, rang doorbells and in summer stole flowers from gardens.

There was no underlying social principle which might have served to unite those living on the avenue. We came to know as we grew up what each adult male worked at, we knew who drank, we knew whose garden we could enter to retrieve a lost ball. But there was no sharing, no one to whom you would be sent for a few spoonfuls of sugar or a half-pound of butter. Community spirit as such did not exist. The front garden, the enclosing wall and the gate on which my father painted the letters 'Shamrock Lodge' each year provided us with a secure haven. And so it was with every one of the forty households on the avenue.

At that time we were probably becoming aware of certain gradations in society which accorded a higher ranking to 'avenue' than to 'street' which, in turn, took precedence over 'lane'. Much later when I came to understand such matters more clearly, I can remember a successful application to the Cork Corporation to change Portney's Lane to Portney's Avenue.

In a world where sports complexes did not exist but where motor-cars were few, the roadway was a playground. Hurling was easily the most popular game and I can't ever remember being without a hurley. When they were broken we 'spliced' them with strips of tin found on tea-chests in a nearby quarry. We did not always have a sliotar but a rubber ball did equally well.

Last Days on the Avenue

No one can recall when childhood ends and another stage of life begins. For me it seems to have been the time when other gardens and more especially other trees in other and bigger gardens were known to have birds' nests. I never became a collector of eggs but enjoyed the excitement of coming upon a nest concealed in a wall or high up on a tree in Jennings's Wood. Jennings's Wood was part of a strip of woodland which must once have covered the southern slopes of the river Lee. The owner, Tom Jennings, was then living in Brookfield on the city side of the wood. We could see the honey-coloured walls of the house when on summer days Frank Crowley and myself made our way stealthily down to the level of the curving river which flowed between the wood and what is now the Cork Greyhound Track. Jennings's Wood was a paradise which we firmly believed was known only to us.

Tom Jennings and his brother Francis owned a very successful mineral water factory in Brown Street which closed only in 1976. Tom had studied in Cambridge where in three successive years he had won the high jump. He later married a daughter of one of Cork's oldest families, the Sarsfields of Doughcloyne.

Frank Crowley was an altar-boy and persuaded me to become one. It had never been my ambition but as it seemed unlikely to interfere with my aim of becoming a tram-driver, I agreed. Thus in my tenth year I became a trainee altar-boy at the Bon Secours Convent and Home on the College Road. It was a rather exclusive appointment as there were but two of us. There were separate chaplains for the Convent and for the Home. Father Tom Duggan, chaplain to the Convent, had served in the First World War as chaplain to the Munster Fusiliers. Some twenty years later he held the same appointment with the Durham Light Infantry and for his services was awarded an MC and an OBE. Apart from the military leaders involved, he was probably the single most important figure in the negotiations which led to the Truce of 1922. It was a tribute to his integrity that although his background was unequivocally Republican, he was accepted by both sides.

Altogether more interesting to us altar-boys was Father John O'Connell, chaplain to the Home. He was completely deaf which meant that he sometimes gave the strangest answers to the questions put to him. He took snuff, which absentmindedly he used to offer us on occasion, and the capacious pockets of his overcoat always seemed to contain small boxes of the locally-made Turkish Delight which from time to time he presented us with.

When I grew older I was entrusted with a special mission about once a month. This brought me to the Reparation Convent on Summerhill South to collect altar-breads for the convent. I liked to preserve great secrecy about this assignment, even altering my route in what I now recognise is the approved secret service method, and always going alone. What added to the sense of mystery was the complete silence in which the whole operation was carried out. The procedure never varied. On arriving at the convent, I placed the biscuit-tin which I carried on a revolving shelf and waited while it was being filled. No sound but the murmur of nuns at prayer came from within. The revolving shelf revolved again. The tin reappeared and I prepared myself for any dangers I might encounter on my return journey.

One episode during my years of service to the Order of Bon Secours may have unsettled the nerves of the nuns for ever. The Feast of the Assumption is marked in the Catholic Church by ceremonies of great splendour. On the Sunday within the Octave, a priest from the Sacred Heart College 'supplied' in the absence of Father Duggan. He was small, round and rubicund.

As he had come to give Benediction, I busied myself lighting the charcoal for the thurible while he was vesting. Sharp on eleven o'clock I trotted out in front of him, resplendent in white surplice and swinging the thurible into which I slipped the odd dollop of incense. The priest mounted the steps to the altar as I knelt down. He turned round almost at once. I then noticed that he was too small to reach the tabernacle where the ciborium containing the host for Exposition of the Blessed Sacrament was kept. I realised his predicament and remembering that O'Connell's, painters and decorators, had been working in the sacristy, I scampered off to get ladders.

On entering the sacristy I was faced with a problem. The ladder resting against the wall was of great length. *Que faire*? I grasped it firmly in the middle and lowered it carefully so that one end fitted through the doorway leading to the chapel. Puffing and blowing I trailed the end of it behind me and emerged into the sanctuary. St Brigid standing on a pedestal on the gospel side of the altar, barely escaped decapitation as I turned to manoeuvre the ladder down the centre aisle. This I had to do if one end was to rest on the altar. As I swivelled round, nuns fled from their stalls and sought safety in the confessional boxes or cowered behind the Reverend Mother. The priest, by this time purple with anger, must have felt himself threatened by the ladder which I was pushing in his direction. He managed to blurt out in a hoarse voice, 'Not that.'

The step-ladder incident was probably in the same year that all those serving in city churches were taken on an excursion to Knockadoon, a stretch of sand on the eastern side of Cork harbour. We travelled by char-à-banc, sitting back to back as we jolted over dusty, pot-holed roads on the solid rimless tyres of those days.

I cannot say with certainty, but this may have been the first time that I saw the sea. It must be borne in mind that even Crosshaven, Cork's nearest seaside resort, was considered to be far from the city in my parents' time, only to be reached on the 'Green Boats'. These steamers, so called because of their colour, left the Albert Quay at stated hours for Crosshaven and later, when the Cork, Blackrock and Passage Railway was built, met passengers from the train at Monkstown and took them to Crosshaven. The service must have been the forerunner of commuter travel and Lennox Robinson recalls his father travelling by Green Boat to and from Cork each day.

The coming of trams, horse-trams in 1872 and electric trams in 1898, brought Cork people to the sea at Blackrock. As children we loved especially the Tivoli-Blackrock route: bells clanged, wheels grated and trolley poles sparked as the tram groaned its way up Dead Woman's Hill before speeding down to Ballintemple and Blackrock. Dead Woman's Hill owes its name to the morgue of a private mental hospital, Linville, which existed at the foot of that hill. It was also a rendezvous for duellists and it was the duty of one of the house surgeons at the nearby South Infirmary to attend the duels which were fought there.

While there are many in Cork who recall the trams, not many people in Ireland or indeed elsewhere had the experience of travelling on the monorail that ran from Listowel to Ballybunion. I was on it at least once when my father brought me with him to his native Kerry on holidays. To say that the train 'ran' is not quite accurate when referring to the 'Lartique', as it was known to be irregular and unpredictable in its behaviour. After scampering along towards Lisselton at a brisk 15 m.p.h, it would appear to lose heart and slow almost to a walking pace.

To ensure that the carriages were balanced, passengers and heavy iron weights were interchangeable. A cow was kept at each terminus to ensure 'ballast' in case a cow, *only one at a time*, had to be carried. Alas, the 'Lartique' 'stopped short never to go again' in 1924.

I do not remember my mother ever accompanying us to Kerry even though she too was born there. I am now inclined to think that she probably enjoyed the freedom which our absence gave her. There was after all the difference in age and, whereas my mother was light-hearted and fun-loving, my father was stern to the point of severity.

He was not always so and while shaving in the morning he would sing snatches from songs associated with his days in the police. One in particular was called 'The Boys of the Old Brigade'. And in the evening when the *Echo* had been read, he would take me on his knee and recite a ballad — always the same — beginning with the words,

> I'll tell you a story about Johnny McGory
> Who went to the wood and killed a tory
> Brought him home and ate his supper
> Went to the wood and killed another.

A verse echoing perhaps the tales he would have heard of Ribbonmen and Whiteboys, the *toraithe* or rapparees who flourished in north Kerry and west Limerick.

My father's years in the RIC must have done much to shape him. Long after 1910, when he retired from the force, he continued to wear an air of authority. In more recent years I have often wondered from whom did he inherit his quite exceptional concern for his appearance. Not too many men, born on small farms in rural Ireland in the last century, could have dressed with the same degree of care that he did.

Sunday morning saw him at his sartorial best. From his carefully waxed moustache to his carefully polished shoes, it is hardly too much to say that he presented to the world the appearance of someone who a few years earlier might have been among the guests at Dublin Castle or the Vice-Regal Lodge in Phoenix Park. A flower in the lapel of his jacket, the corner of a handkerchief showing in the breast-pocket, together with a coloured waistcoat, must have given him the assurance that he was the best-dressed man on the avenue as, selecting his silver-topped cane from the hallstand, he set off for his Sunday walk.

As I trotted dutifully beside him, he would make sure that I walked with my shoulders held well back. Only years later did I chance to discover whence came this insistence on 'shoulders well back'. A Garda sergeant named McGrath was widely known as 'Thumbs'. He drilled new recruits at the Depot and saw to it that they inserted their thumbs into the tiny sachets sewn into the arms of the uniform which compelled them to march with their shoulders held back. Was this, I wonder, a relic of the RIC?

Our walks did not vary greatly. Down to the end of the avenue where I was entrusted with a three-penny piece to give to the shawled woman who was always to be found on Sunday mornings at the top of the Gaol Walk. Then out past Westcourt where the Misses Bergin might be seen playing croquet, past the Bon Secours Home and up the slope to Dennehy's Cross.

All beyond was open country but another hill or two had to be faced before we reached Lehane's of the Rock Farm where we always turned back. From time to time I was lifted up on a wall to admire the crops. My father had inherited instincts that were in tune to pastoral life, to the changes that the seasons bring, to seedtime and harvest. He never really lost his love of fields and much of my own love of the countryside I owe to him.

An uncle of mine who was also in the RIC told me that even when on furlough, my father insisted on maintaining a high standard of dress . He used an expression to describe him which is far more vivid in the Irish from which it is derived. He was, he said, as 'picked' (*piocaithe*: smart, well turned-out) as when on parade.

Even though my mother lived long after him, his influence on me is I think much greater. Breaches of discipline have always been for me matters calling for punishment. In this I must resemble him. I once saw him catch a youth who was stealing apples and march him down to the police-barracks. On another occasion when bowl players on the Model Farm Road threw the bowl dangerously near where we were walking, my father picked up the bowl and slung it far into a field of corn.

He must have been something of an athlete as he treasured a medal for the hop-step-and-jump, and a photo which for long hung over the fireplace in the kitchen showed him in an RIC tug-of-war team of 1891.

He had been ill for some time before his death and was a patient at Dr Barter's Hydro in Blarney in the early months of 1926. He died at home and was 'waked' in the room where he died. Friends, relatives and nuns from the Bon Secours convent recited prayers and replaced one another in the room throughout the night.

On the following day, during which blinds in all the houses on the avenue remained drawn, his body was brought to 'the Lough' church. Passers-by crossed themselves or walked *trí coiscéim na trócaire* as the hearse went by. On the third day his funeral took place to St Finbarr's Cemetery.

Custom ordained that on the death of a husband the widow wore black for the following six months and I can remember accompanying my mother to McKechnie's in Sharman Crawford Street to have costumes and suits dyed. In earlier times widows would continue to wear black until the end of their days.

My regret is that after his death all relations with his people in Kerry seem to have been severed and I grew up knowing nothing of them. Some may have emigrated but the only one of my parents' immediate relations who I know had emigrated was my mother's only brother. He went to Canada after being dismissed from the Lee Boot Factory in Washington Street for smoking, or so it was alleged. Even in exile a link with Cork turned up when he found himself in lodgings in Toronto with a man named Allman whose family owned a distillery in Bandon.

Easily my favourite among my relations was an uncle by marriage whose behaviour occasionally bordered on eccentricity.

He resembled the grandfather in Henri Bordeaux's novel *La Maison* who affected to despise private property and held religion in mild contempt. When we went for a walk together, which we often did after my father's death, he would walk through private gardens and tramp unconcernedly across fields marked 'Trespassers will be prosecuted'. This made him something of a hero in my eyes, especially when we helped ourselves to apples in an orchard.

Oddly enough, for someone who as an RIC sergeant had spent most of his life upholding law and order, he would talk of robbers as if they were benefactors of society. He was cynically dismissive of all politicians, sometimes muttering to himself apropos nothing or no one in particular, 'Ireland a nation, the land for the people, hold the harvest'. When in company and pressed for a song, he would give out an old 'Come all Ye', remembered from his boyhood in Lisronagh, which had as its refrain:

> This is the way the wheel is turning
> Rolling on from day to day;
> Norwood dead across in England
> Carey shot upon the say.

Another uncle by marriage, Charles McCarthy, was a singer with but one song, Denny Lane's 'Carrigdhoun'. He was born on the sloping hillside above Céim Carraige Bridge beneath which a stream from Ballinreeshig Glen flows down to the Owenabuee, the river immortalised in the song.

Life in the City Centre

In the summer of 1926 we moved from Highfield Avenue and went to live at 95 North Main Street over the business premises of Uncle Charles. He was a plumber and the men whom he employed, Chandler, Cody, Moriarty and Connolly, all wore bowler hats which I came to associate with the trade. He had been a racing cyclist and at this time owned a powerful two-stroke Indian motor-cycle which signalled his coming long before he arrived at 8 o'clock every morning to take down the shutters on the shop.

The North Main Street was then the heartland of shopping in the city where shawled women, their stalls piled high with fruit, vegetables and dulse, did a busy trade. Yet three pawnbroking shops in the length of that short street pointed to the existence of much poverty in the twenties. Food such as drisheen (a Cork delicacy made of oatmeal and sheep's blood, flavoured with herbs), tripe and crubeens were not sold on open stalls but from covered stalls on Cornmarket Street or in the English Market on the Grand Parade.

I enjoyed living in a place which seemed to come to life each evening when, by contrast, Highfield Avenue would have been asleep. In summertime the street tended to become an extended concert hall after the public houses had closed and when the customers, reluctant to return home, sang in something approaching harmony until midnight.

Amid the noise and traffic of that busy thoroughfare is the Church of St Peter's, now in a ruinous condition. Fronting it is a neglected patch of grass, a lone elm tree and a few lichened tombstones. There, during the years when I lived beside it, an old man was to be seen each summer mowing the grass with a scythe. It was a scene little different from that described by Dickens in

'The City of the Absent' where he tells of an old man and woman whom he saw making hay in the heart of London, 'Yes, of all occupations in the world, making hay!'

The couple whom Dickens watched had 'but one rake between them, and they both had hold of it in a pastorally-loving manner, and there was hay on the old woman's black bonnet, as if the old woman had recently been playful. The old man was quite an obsolete old man, in knee-breeches and coarse grey stockings and the old woman wore mittens like unto his stockings in texture and colour.'

And there they worked under what Dickens, as though to lay stress on the miniature he had painted, called 'three and a half yards of darkening sky'.

Off the North Main Street is Kyle Street, which was then and still is a great emporium of old clothes. In my time upwards of a score of second-hand dealers laid out their stocks of clothes, furniture and hardware in that short narrow street while round the corner on the quay, Maggie Murphy sat behind a cobwebbed window in front of mounds of books. Another Maggie, known as 'Maggie the Watergrass', who was always barefooted, sold watercress from a basket on the streets and sometimes from a stall on the North Gate Bridge.

On the other side of the North Main Street, tradesmen and craft workers were to be found in Grattan Street, part of the reclaimed 'Marsh'. Probably not as many as in the previous century when we are told that 'metal workers, farriers, harness makers, tinsmiths, and coppersmiths' lived in the handsome houses that lay between the Courthouse and the river and also in Piccadilly Lane and Cockpit Lane.

This tendency to group together those linked by an identity of interests was slow to extend to the professions, but gradually the Harley Street of Cork, which had once been the South Mall, moved up to Patrick's Hill. While no statistics are available, the dangers of coronary thrombosis must have been considerably increased by the time the doctor's patients arrived gasping and panting after climbing even part of that steep hill.

While the orthodox medical practitioners were to be found on the hill and in Patrick's Place, Mr Lane, an osteopath or as he was generally known 'the bone man', held clinics in nearby MacCurtain Street. He was highly regarded by country people and he visited all the county towns on a regular basis.

Solicitors seemed to have congregated on the South Mall almost from the time that this tree-lined thoroughfare which was Dunscome's Marsh was covered over in the eighteenth century. John Boyle, editor of the *Cork Freeholder* (1820), referred to them in less than flattering terms as having 'spread themselves on the South Mall like crocodiles on the banks of the Nile'.

The red and white sugar-stick symbols of the barber's trade were to be found in almost every city street. These have always been the great 'clearing houses' for gossip of all kinds and there was one such repository of information within a few yards of the North Main Street. Tim Horgan's barber's shop provided up-dated information on the current form of horses, greyhounds, racing pigeons, ferrets and beagles. He also 'made a book' on each day's racing and, as he was not a licensed bookmaker, you paid no tax whether you won or lost.

A haircut cost fourpence and as value for money with no refinements it was unbeatable. Tim cut every rib of hair down to the roots with the exception of a dozen or so which were left, presumably to mark where the forehead began and the scalp ended. He then sprayed the stubble with some powerful aromatic liquid which had the local bees sending out signals to distant hives that Tim Horgan's was the place to be.

He liked to recall the victory of Timothy II, a horse of which he was part owner, at Cork Park races on Easter Sunday, 1913. In the steeplechase event there were but two horses engaged; Charlemagne, ridden by Henry Latham and Timothy II, ridden by Jack Murphy. At the fence in front of the grandstand, Timothy II fell and his jockey was injured. Jack's brother, Tom, ran on to the course, caught the horse and, wearing his ordinary clothes, rode him to victory.

The result was disputed by Latham on the grounds of the winning jockey's weight but the stewards upheld the result as Tom Murphy weighed in *over* the weight which his brother was carrying.

My own association with 'the Sport of Kings' was less happy. Glocamorra is the name of a townland on the Cork side of Mitchelstown where the road swings high over the moorland towards Ballindangan. A song called 'Glocamorra' was popular in the forties especially among Cork exiles in Dagenham when, tired of belting out 'Thady Quill' and 'The Holy Ground', something more sentimental was called for. So, when I saw that a horse called 'Glocamorra' was running at Phoenix Park, I took five shillings from my mother's purse and placed it on him. Alas, 'Glocamorra', worried no doubt by the extent of his responsibility, dropped dead in the course of the race.

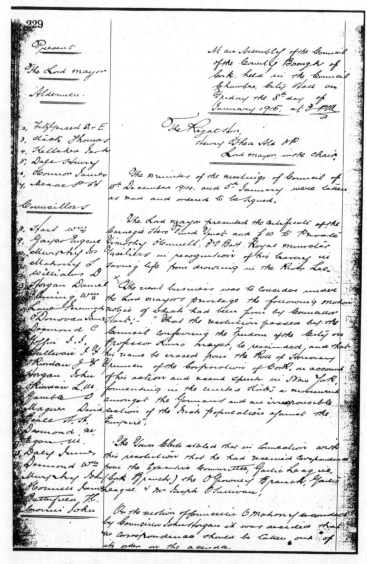

Minutes of Cork Corporation, January 1915

A new School and new Friends

The duration of school-going in the 'twenties depended almost entirely on money. I realise that it still does but to a somewhat lesser extent. If, after the age of twelve, your parents were able to afford the fees at secondary school, you continued on to sit the Intermediate Certificate examination after four years, and the Leaving Certificate examination after a further two. There were some scholarships on offer to primary school pupils but very few — ten County Council scholarships for the entire county of Cork!

I sat the scholarship examination at the Model School in Anglesea Street and I remember the occasion largely because of what later befell the examiner in oral Irish. He was Mr Kirwan, a Divisional Inspector with the Department of Education, and he was later shot dead while on inspection at the Vocational School in Hospital, County Limerick. I remembered him as being very kind to me when he realised that I was the last candidate to be examined that day.

I failed to win a scholarship but with several other boys from Glasheen School, I entered Presentation College on the Western Road in September 1926. The college was staffed almost entirely by monks of the Order, very different from the position today when, in its new surroundings on the Mardyke and with a greatly increased number of pupils, lay teachers are very much in the majority.

The headmaster was Brother Connolly, known to all as 'the Man'. His sight was said to be failing and he was believed to see objects only if they moved. Within the first few weeks of my arrival, I tested this belief. I had absented myself from class and he came looking for me. I stood motionless in the corridor as he emerged from a room and came towards me. He did not hesitate but took me by the ear and led me back to my classroom. All doubts about his eyesight were banished from my mind. He took Religious Instruction or, as it was entered on the timetable, 'Apologetics'. It did not really matter what it was called as it consisted of his interminable accounts of the careers of old boys who had passed through the Royal Military College at Sandhurst and gone on to rule the British Empire as officials of the Indian Civil Service. As they all seemed to have become Viceroys, we imagined India as being governed exclusively by Pres boys who talked of Delhi as if it was an extension of 'de Dyke', and the Royal Bengal Lancers became as well-known to us as the 1st Cork Brigade. Names of hill stations such as Rawalpindi and Peshawar were as familiar to us as the Kerry Pike and in our conversation we would sometimes refer casually to 'tiffin' when others still spoke of tea.

The departure of the British after the Treaty was ratified must have had its effect on the school curriculum but the success rate of the school's Old Boys remained unaffected. Instead of manning distant outposts of the Empire, the new examinations led them to accept appointments nearer home. William Carey became Chairman of the Revenue Commissioners, Nicholas Nolan became Secretary to the Government, Sean Collins-Powell, Adjutant-General of the Army, Frank Gallagher, Editor of the *Irish Press*, Tim O'Driscoll, Director-General of Bord Fáilte, while two members of the McCarthy clan were appointed to the Judiciary.

As a young man, Frank Gallagher had worked as a reporter of the Commons debates for the *Cork Free Press*. He was dismissed for failing to give the correct figure for an important division in the House. He was under the impression that a member with a double-barrelled name was two people! His career did not, however, end there. Before becoming the first editor of the *Irish Press*, he edited the *Free Press* and wrote extensively under the name of David Hogan.

Sean O'Faolain had left Pres before my arrival but I corresponded with him after a Senior Inspector of Schools, John Bithrey, had read one of his short stories to a 6th year class as an example of a superb short story. The story had been published in *The Listener* and I wrote to O'Faolain telling him of the accolade

Munster Fusiliers leaving Glanmire terminus — off to the war (1914-18).

My father in RIC uniform.

Jim Cadan, my first cousin.

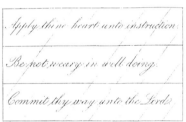

Copper plate headlines from a
Vere Foster copybook —
always of an improving
nature.

Frank Crowley and myself as
altarboys. In those days
surplices were worn only
once, then whisked off to be
washed and starched.

Delivery van of the Cork and Kerry Creamery Company.

Head office of Sutton's coal firm, South Mall.

OVERLEAF:
Snowball fight at the bandstand on the Mardyke.
Outdoor concerts were then more common than today.

Crosshaven looking towards Currabinny.

Connie Doyle with the Fair Hill Harriers. He was famous far beyond Fair Hill for his dog Ringwood, known as the 'armoured car'.

The Rebel City, c. 1930.

RAF flying-boat at Haulbowline (1936).

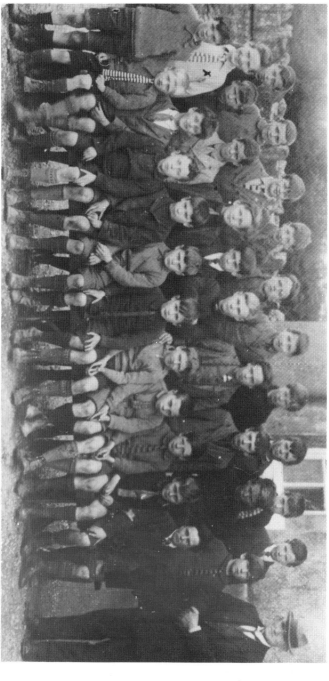

Fifth class, Glasheen National School, 1924. My mother was clearly determined that I would be easily identified' (marked with an ×). If memory serves me, the class is as follows: *Back row*: E. Hipwell, M. O'Shea, M. Attwood, B. Curtis, T. Dempsey, M. Walsh, J. Crowley, T. Horgan, J. Kirby, T. McCarthy. *Middle row*: T. McElligott, G. Exall, H. Spillett, D. Cotter, M. O'Mahony, T. Hayes, D. Conway, P. Sheehan, C. Carey, M. Conway. *Front row*: J. McSwiney, H. Mercer, M. Buckley, T. O'Driscoll, J. Young, M. Riordan, J. Finnegan, B. McKenna, D. McCarthy, A. McTighe, B. Donovan, J. Fahy.

accorded by Bithrey. Back came a postcard thanking me and adding the delightful curtain line, 'Every circus pony likes his lump of sugar and I liked mine'.

Brother Connolly's influence in matters educational was considerable and on his recommendation four of his staff, O'Donnell, Wall, Fitzgerald, and Sean Connolly, were appointed inspectors. Fitzgerald was left in no doubt as to why he was being recommended: 'You will never make a teacher so you had better become an inspector,' was Brother Connolly's dubious comment.

The Presentation Brothers never enjoyed the same reputation as the Christian Brothers for helping the national cause but they did make their own contribution. Paddy O'Keeffe, later to become General Secretary of the GAA, had taught in their school on Lancaster Quay. Years later, while 'on the run' during the Black and Tan war, he was sheltered by the Brothers and shared their community life at Mount St Joseph's. And it was garbed as a monk that he crossed through military check-points to another safe refuge, the Fire Station on Sullivan's Quay.

Classes at Pres began at nine o'clock but the gates were opened by Denis Buckley, the caretaker, at eight o'clock. Those of us with homework to complete were invariably among the early arrivals and I used leave the house soon after eight o'clock and dash through Peter's Church Lane, across Grattan Street and up Sheares Street. If I got in early I might get a game of handball, a game at which two of the teachers, Fitzgerald and Connolly, excelled.

There was then no secondary school for boys in such towns as Ballincollig, Bandon, Carrigaline and Kinsale. This meant that Pres, like all other city schools, had a high proportion of 'country' pupils in each class. They came in waves, some on the Irish Omnibus Company's buses, some by the Muskerry train and others by bicycle.

For reasons that may have something to do with its name, Pres has always attracted far more Jews than did Christian College. Such names as Scher, Sandler, Sless, Sayers, Goldberg, Jackson, Newman, Beare and Rosehill occur frequently in the class-lists of the late 'twenties. We never thought of them in terms of the racist stereotype of the Jew as money-lender, nor was I ever aware of any prejudice against them. There were then a few hundred Jews in Cork, most of them very able businessmen and, not surprisingly, many musicians and painters of high quality.

It is customary to say that schooldays are happy days. Apart from being compelled to study mathematics, I enjoyed my five years at Pres. Logarithms I particularly disliked and I could never make anything of the little figures standing on what appeared to be the right shoulder of the digit. On the day of the Matriculation examination a ripple of laughter ran through the hall when the Supervisor was seen to hand me a copy of the log tables. It was the general impression that a railway timetable would have proved little less helpful to me.

In my last year I shared a 'front-line' desk with Bill Hegarty and Bobby McCarthy where any inattention or idleness was unlikely to pass unnoticed. At one time we decided to keep a record of the number of days when we escaped punishment. It stayed at zero and we gave up.

Bill cycled the eight miles from his home in Waterfall each day and sometimes, particularly on warm afternoons, he would put his head down and nod off. One day when his frame fairly vibrated to the rhythm of his gentle snores, the geography teacher, Kevin Harty, spotted him, shook him and said, 'Time to get up' whereupon Bill shot up muttering, 'Where's my shirt?'

When we got a new teacher it was decided that I should suffer from myopia and a lisp. This dual affliction would, or so I was assured, ensure my exemption from almost all work in the new teacher's classes. All went well on that first day until I was asked a question on Greenland. 'Gweenland,' I began 'is a gweat countwy ....' I got no further in that sentence. A shadow loomed over me. 'Repeat that sentence,' said the shadow. Brother Dermot who was teaching in the next classroom had come in. The spectacles which I had been loaned because of my 'myopia' dropped and I found myself repeating in an eager voice, 'Greenland is a great country ....' I was cured.

While none of the teachers were sensationally bad, there was an uneven quality in the teaching. Religious communities seemed to assume that each member of the Order was competent to teach. In the case of the Presentation Brothers this might mean that some brother who had spent years in a foreign country was, on his return, given a subject to teach whether or not he was qualified in that subject or indeed qualified at all. What now surprises me is the uncritical acceptance amounting almost to veneration with which we noted what the teacher told us. Never a word of protest, only rarely a hand raised to seek an explanation.

Our English teacher in fifth year, Brother Berchmans, freshly returned from Montreal, was quite taken by my seeming familiarity with even the least-known of Shakespeare's plays, not aware that I composed some of my own 'quotations'. These he occasionally read to the class, including one which I myself rather liked! It went like this, 'Dost thou not like our courtly life? / Is it too full of earthly strife?'

The teaching of Irish was in the able hands of Brother Dermot. His methods differed greatly from those of my teachers at the National School and it was quite a change, especially for urban schoolboys, to be faced with the *Slí an Eolais* of Cormac Ó Cadhlaigh in which we learned a great deal of lore associated with the Irish countryside.

One class in Presentation College may be said to have differed from all others. This was the Bank Class. It was the lotus-land where the pupils shunned the honours that might have been theirs had they sat for 'the Junior Ex' or won a Honan Scholarship. Theirs was an uncomplicated existence, lightened by midmorning visits to Campbell's shop to enjoy, when funds permitted, a De Reszke cigarette, 'the ten-minute smoke for intelligent folk', or, if one is to believe gossip of the time, a visit to licensed premises in Sheares Street.

Most of the pupils were being crammed for the Munster and Leinster Bank examination but the course catered for those intended for all banks — National, Provincial, Hibernian, etc. They came to Pres not alone from distant parts of County Cork but from all the counties of Munster.

Once, to the stupefaction of the entire Bank Class, a pupil announced his intention of moving back to the ordinary Leaving Certificate class. Such a decision was difficult to understand. Why should anyone voluntarily exchange the undisturbed tranquillity, which was the norm of life in the Bank Class, for one of serious study in any other? It was thought that the aberration was but momentary and that he would return. His friends reasoned with him and sought to make him renounce what they considered folly. To no avail. He went on to take the Leaving Certificate with honours, entered the Civil Service and later became a High Court judge in Hong Kong.

The fame of the Bank Class rested on one man, Tim O'Donoghue, known as 'Beetroot'. Indeed, most of the overdrafts of Cork's citizens must at one time or another have been in the hands of his former pupils. A native of Banteer and at one time a university lecturer in mathematics, he was revered as much for his wit as for his wisdom.

As well as being a noted teacher, Tim was a rugby enthusiast. None of those then at school are likely to forget the memorable evening in 1926 when, after returning from Limerick where they had won the Munster Schools Cup, the victorious team and supporters gathered at 'the Statue'. There Tim, his face incandescent in the gaslight, sang a victory song which he had composed in the train on the way back. It was sung to the air of 'Mademoiselle from Armentières' and commemorated in particular the exploits of the captain, Jim O'Leary, who scored two tries.

As a public-spirited citizen and as chairman of the Cork County Council, he joined the Local Defence Force (LDF) during 'the Emergency'. His duties entailed the night-patrolling of an area which ran from Orrery Hill at the top of Blarney Street to Faggot Hill on the old road to Blarney. He was on duty one night when he noticed a light going on and off in a distant field. Convinced that a parachutist had landed (one had landed the previous week in county Clare), Tim hurried to report to the nearest police barracks, North Abbey on the North Mall.

When he arrived breathless, he found the barracks closed but an upstairs window opened and a garda looked out. 'What's up?' he shouted. 'A parachutist has landed above on Blarney Road.' 'Put salt on his tail' was the reply and the window closed.

The strength of the Local Defence Force was reduced by one in the course of the following twenty-four hours but the 'lamping' of rabbits on the Blarney Road was unaffected.

If I have a criticism to offer of the Pres of my time, it is that the curriculum was so limited — no visual arts, no modern languages, no metalwork or woodwork. Pupils were fed on a diet that ensured examination success. That they did succeed, the results of each year testified. Intermediate Certificate scholarships, Leaving Certificate scholarships, Honan scholarships, university entrance scholarships, all came their way. And for such services to education, the headmaster, Brother Connolly, was awarded an honorary doctorate by the Senate of the National University in 1927.

When, however, criticism has had its say, it must be borne in mind that schooling is always a reflection of the age and that secondary schooling for all was undreamt of when in the nineteenth century such schools as Pres and Christians first opened their doors. There is no doubt that neither school made any effort to open its doors to the less well-off sections of the community by offering scholarships, nor did either school seek to expand the curriculum beyond high-marked examination subjects.

Presentation College and Christian College were 'the flagships' of the two Orders in Cork. Fees were high. My mother paid three or four pounds each term. Each Order had, however, other schools in the city where only nominal fees if any were charged, notably the North Monastery (Christian) and the South Monastery (Presentation). We may also be sure that within the Orders there was discussion on the question of 'making educational provision for the poor' which was central to the teaching of their common founder, Ignatius Rice.

Farranferris, the diocesan college for the diocese of Cork, has never seemed to attain the same degree of importance as similar colleges elsewhere in Ireland. It remained in some way remote, perched on a hillside above the city but not in any way associated with the educational life of the city. This may of course be due to the fact that it is chiefly a boarding college with few day pupils. It would I feel bring it closer to the community if it were moved to a campus in the city centre, away from the cold and rather intimidating brick building which it occupies and which dates back to 1887. There are sites in Cornmarket Street, Paul Street and the Marsh where, in the midst of dwelling-houses and shops, priests and students might share in the ordinary life of the city.

Both Pres and Christians seemed satisfied to perpetuate a selective system based on the 'superior schools' idea popularised by the Commissioners of Intermediate Education. The supposed superiority was based on the teaching of Greek and Latin while such irrelevant skills as modern languages were, in consequence, ignored. Music, when taught at all, was obviously considered to be an unnecessary addition to the pupil's knowledge. At Pres, drawing was taught as an extra by Bill Sheehy, a well-loved teacher, who was paid by the hour. Sadly, I cannot recall a single painting on the walls of classroom or corridor, the absence of which must have a desolating effect on the imagination of the young.

In part explanation of the 'conservation' of Pres, I would say that the Victorian age with its solid moral framework and its belief in class structure lingered on in Cork after it had been displaced elsewhere. Generations had accepted the primacy of Pres and Christians as schools for the elite, with 'the Mon' and 'Sully's Quay' for the others. There was a sort of passive acceptance of this arrangement and the splendid diversity of education seemed not to touch the citizens.

Fortunately, human intelligence does not respect social attitudes and one of Frank O'Connor's short stories, entitled 'Old Fellows', contains a revealing passage:

'The north side of the city,' said the sailor, '. . . what is it only foreigners? People that came in from beyond the lamps a generation ago. Tramps and fiddlers and pipers.'

'They had the intellect,' said my da quietly . . . cocking his head at the sailor.

'Intellect?' said the sailor. 'The north side?'

''Twas always given up to them,' said my da with a sniff.'

The social cleavage that school represented was reflected even on the sportsfield. Both Pres and Christians are today rugby strongholds, disdaining any link with the traditional game of hurling. It wasn't always so and I must be one of the few who can recall the year 1927 when Pres won the Munster Cup both in hurling and rugby. That was the climax of four successive years in which Pres won the Cork Schools Cup in senior hurling. After that, bourgeois gentility triumphed and apart from an isolated effort in 1932 when Pres fielded a team against Farranferris, the shutters may be said to have gone up on hurling.

The hurlers and rugby players of 1926/27 deserve to be remembered: T.J. O'Driscoll, J. O'Leary, P. Fogarty, N. McAuliffe, Phil O'Sullivan, J.J. O'Callaghan, W. Nunan, T. McCarthy, Paddy O'Sullivan, W. Twomey, J. Glynn, D. Nagle, F. Hegarty, J. O'Sullivan.

Of these I remember best Noel McAuliffe who in our eyes rivalled C.B. Fry as an example of an all-round sportsman. Noel played rugby for Munster, Free State League soccer with Bohemians, hurling for Pres and cricket for Cork County.

On my last day at Pres I sat in the window embrasure of the old Physics Lab where it overlooked the Western Road. I was with Dick Cantillon from Carrigaline and we were both somewhat sad, something we would have thought highly unlikely some months or even days before. It was as though all the days spent in the school were sunlit, happy ones. Perhaps they were.

We sat disconsolately there, idly watching the shafts of sunlight dance on the bell-jars and flasks and reflect the colour of the butterflies' wings in the glass case over the door. Through the screen of laurel leaves we saw boys and girls with togs going for a swim in the open-air baths at the Lee Fields while across the river small puffs of smoke marked where the Muskerry train was putting up steam for its westward journey.

The scene from the window was part of a pattern, the last threads of which had been woven for us when Brother Evangelist, Brother Berchmans, Brother Dermot, Kevin Harty and Dan Duggan took farewell of us. Such schoolboy delights as swims at Long Reach and Lakelands, matinees at the Assembly Rooms, ice-creams at Macari's — these, all these, were about to end. No more would we tumble down the steps from the tea-rooms or flee from the simulated wrath of the caretaker as with shouts of 'Six o'clock. Come on, out now. Home to your tea' ringing in our ears, Denis drove us home. Never again would we listen to Evangelist's doleful forecasts of what would happen to us if we did not study and his insistence that only by doing so would we avoid ending up in the Workhouse on the Douglas Road.

City Life

I n the year that I left Pres my mother remarried and we moved from the North Main Street to live in No.1 Waterloo Place off the Wellington Road. It was a high rambling house with what was a sort of private road in front which separated the house from an extensive garden. To reach the house from the main road, one climbed some sixty steps and to reach my room I climbed four flights of stairs! I never liked the house but I was to live there for three years.

It is difficult to imagine how, within the boundaries of what was then a small city, two such contrasting places as Wellington Road and the North Main Street could be found. The North Main Street with its pawnshops and pubs, clothes dealers, ballad singers and beggars was full of life from dawn to dusk. Wellington Road, by contrast, was withdrawn and sedate, conscious of a certain faded dignity that found shelter behind fringed lampshades and heavily-lined curtains.

Even the names one met with were redolent of the past — Clarence Place, Empress Place, Adelaide Terrace. Names that one might expect to find in a quiet seaside town in the south of England. It seemed that in Ireland, as the hold of the Empire on her subjects weakened, a certain sentimental attachment to imperial links strengthened.

Nothing marked so clearly this divide in Cork society as church-going on a Sunday morning. The different congregations fell into easily defined categories. For style and an air of unobtrusive elegance, those who attended service in the Wesleyan Church in Patrick Street were outstanding. The congregation at St Peter and Paul's Catholic Church did well, though admittedly in a more subdued style. Good suits and well-polished shoes pointed to business success rather than to inherited wealth. St Augustine's in Washington Street was looked on more as a popular point of assembly for those who, in something of a hurry, were going off after ten-thirty Mass to fish on the Lee at Inniscarra or further west at Dripsey.

Lovers of good church singing, and there were many such in Cork, favoured the twelve o'clock mass at St Mary's on Pope's Quay. Some great voices were to be heard in that choir gallery — Jimmie Cowhie, Harry Whitehouse, Tim Healy — all good enough to have received invitations from the Carl Rosa Opera Company to sing professionally. Flintoff Moore, who sang with that company, would often come, when they were playing at the Opera House, to sing a solo at the twelve o'clock mass at St Peter and Paul's.

Whatever the merits of church choirs, no Corkman called on to sing 'a few bars' would ever refuse the challenge even of the most inaccessible notes in the most complicated arias. Such devotion to song may account for the popularity of the Celebrity Concerts which attracted thousands to the Savoy Cinema in the 'thirties to hear Richard Tauber singing 'Yew are my Heart's Deelight' and Paul Robeson singing 'Ole Man River'.

Many of these aspirants to the glory of 'La Scala' were members of the Butter Exchange Band, known as 'the Butterah', or the Barrack Street Band, known as 'the Barrackah', to us the most celebrated musical ensembles in the country. As a child I had heard tales of the fearsome followers of the Fair Lane Fife and Drum Band who, when they marched towards the South Gate Bridge, gave rise to the warning cry 'Take in your linnets, here's down Fair Lane'.

More peaceful times followed and on a momentous occasion in 1948 the Barrack Street band was invited to the Butter Exchange headquarters. On that Sunday morning, the windows in the upstairs room at No 7 John Redmond Street were wide open so as to hear the approaching band. As both were brass and reed bands, critical ears were turned to judge the quality of the playing. On reaching Dominick Street, the Barrack Street band swung to the right and drew up on the cobbled square where they gave a recital before entering the bandroom for what the newspaper reporter termed 'the customary refreshments'.

Band recitals were given at the bandstand on the Mardyke and on the Marina and, after it was rebuilt, in the City Hall. Singing with the Army Band on one occasion in the 'thirties was Pat

McCormack. Pat, whose real name was Callanan, had sung extensively in Britain, including the Albert Hall, before returning to his native Cork where he became a familiar sight as he walked through the streets always accompanied by his lion cub.

There is a theory to which I do not subscribe that an interest in music is linked with a talent for dancing. False, I say. Nanette Healy, who held dancing classes at her home on the Grand Parade and was known to have a high success rate among the *jeunesse dorée* of the city, found it an impossible task to get my feet to harmonise with the music. When I did find myself in such *palais de danse* as the Arcadia or the Oratory on St Mary's Road, it was as an observer rather than a participant.

My failure on the dance floor, a disability which I shared with the subject of a popular music-hall song, 'Teaching McFadden to Dance', did not seriously inhibit my social life. First of all, only rarely did we on the north side make any romantic forays across the river. The result was that while schoolgirls from 'North Pres' and St Angela's were within our preserves, those from 'South Pres' and 'St Als' were not. Only Patrick Street presented a common meeting ground for the youthful Montagues and Capulets.

I have mentioned the Oratory. To say that it was exclusive is to fail to appreciate how difficult it was to gain entry. By comparison the royal enclosure at Ascot was easily breached, nor was admission to the *Académie Française* more coveted. Cards were issued which gave one right of entry. How I came by one I no longer remember. Was it my service as an altarboy, my godparents in religion, my second place in the Apologetics examination?

Dancing was controlled by the Sisters of Charity and there on a Sunday evening, after Devotions, some extremely decorous dancing was not only permitted but encouraged. Fortunate were those who on a Monday morning could boast that they had danced with the girl of their dreams within the permitted degree of propinquity, which was estimated to be about six inches!

The evening was considered to be a success if one succeeded in persuading the girl to come to a matinee performance in the Assembly Rooms on the following Saturday. The Assembly Rooms specialised in films which we referred to as 'folly-er ups' where each instalment ended dramatically with the heroine bound hand and foot on the railway line as the express thundered towards her. The cinema made no pretensions to luxury but the fourpence which we clutched did guarantee us a seat on a hard chair.

During the summer of 1931 I attended Colburn's Academy on the South Terrace where I took a course in shorthand. My mother's hope was that by doing so, I would be able to take extensive notes when I went to university in the autumn. Despite the efforts of my teacher, Miss Buckley, I made little progress. The distraction of seeing girls in the class was too much for me and all I succeeded in achieving were some shorthand outlines unknown to Mr Pitman.

Far more entertaining if equally unproductive were the art classes at the Sharman Crawford School of Art in Emmet Place where I went on scholarship, worth if I remember five shillings! My art work was to prove a disappointment to my teachers, Miss O'Flaherty and Mr Lee, and my Christmas test earned the disapproving comment 'Little evidence of artistic ability'. So it was that I was never able to avail of the munificence of the Cork-born Joseph Stafford Gibson who, on his death in 1910, left a considerable sum of money (£15,000) for the purchase of paintings and to enable promising students to be sent abroad.

At that time the headmaster was Hugh Charde who had a studio on the Grand Parade and who as a young student had studied in Belgium. Better known was Marshall Hutson who enjoyed the distinction of having had his work exhibited in the Royal Academy and in the Royal Hibernian Academy in the same year. He was then living in Rochestown and one of his paintings, 'Morning Majesty', recalls the glory of a grove of lime trees which once lined the road leading to Monfield House.

When seeking an excuse for going out after tea instead of doing homework, nothing was more likely to allay any doubts my mother may have had than to say that I was going to 'the Loft'. This was the home of the Cork Shakespearian Company situated almost under the shadow of Shandon. The principal actors and actresses were all known to us and when we went to the Opera House for a performance, it was to recognise and applaud familiar figures. And so it must have been in the London of Shakespeare's day when the players at the Globe Theatre were to be met within the coffee-houses and taverns adjoining the Strand.

Almost all the Cork company worked in the city and while none were ostlers at stage doors, the variety of their occupations would surely have delighted Shakespeare. Of those in our own home at Waterloo Place all except Sheila, who was married with a young family, acted on the stage. Gus Healy was a dental mechanic with Eric Scher, his brother Teddy was a foreman at Ford's, while Theresa was a hairdresser with Paddy Parnell on the South Mall.

Anyone eager to join the Company was rarely if ever auditioned. Father O'Flynn, who founded it, was for long attached to the Cathedral parish and it was his custom, when having heard confessions on a Saturday evening, to walk down Mulgrave Road. He would stop and talk to those whom he met and inevitably some of them would walk back with him to 'the Loft'. He might then encourage them to take part in rehearsals and many who were later to make their careers on screen as well as on stage had their first introduction to the theatre in that upstairs room.

I never knew him well, though I did attend rehearsals, but those who did never failed to pay tribute to his remarkable gifts. He paused one evening when I was there to speak of the importance of accent and of its value in revealing character. I cannot recall all or indeed much of what he said but he did emphasise how important accent is to a playwright. He stressed that the Cork accent, like all others, depends on inflexion and intonation to convey a wide range of human emotions. He had us listen to recordings of the same poem read by different readers and welcomed our comments. I have since felt that RTE is at fault when it gives insufficient care to the choice of reader for stories by such writers as O'Connor and O'Faolain, where dialogue plays a significant part in the tale.

Other Shakespearian companies, notably those of Sir Frank Benson and Charles Doran, appeared at the Opera House from time to time. These professional companies never equalled the achievement of the Cork company who in 1928 presented eight Shakespearian plays in the course of one week! To appreciate what this meant, it must be remembered that all were amateurs. One of Father O'Flynn's 'apprentice players' was Edward Mulhall from High Street who began his career as understudy to Jim Stack as the Demon King in the first Opera House pantomime. Mulhall went to Hollywood where, after being given the leading role in 'My Fair Lady', he starred in the series 'The Ghost and Mrs Muir'.

While it is now generally assumed that anyone over the age of sixty-five was a 'regular' at the Opera House, that is only partly true. At the time when I was growing up, the cinema had begun to play a more important part in our lives. I do however remember sitting with my mother in the Back Stalls waiting for the magic moment when the great curtain would rise on a Gilbert and Sullivan operetta with Cork's Percy Diamond and Fan Cottrell as the leading singers.

When the Opera House did go up in flames in 1956, 'a candle of memories was forever quenched'. The fire prompted Bernard Levin, writing in, I think, the *Sunday Times*, to remark on what he called 'the absolute unparalleled record of inflammability' of opera houses. Among those he listed as having burned down were Covent Garden, the Prague Opera, the Berlin Staatsoper, Hamburg, Dresden and Shakespeare's Globe Theatre.

If a box at the Opera House marked the zenith of success for the merchant princes of the city, there were other halls where a discriminating audience acclaimed international celebrities. Among these were the Clarence Hall in the Imperial Hotel, the Savoy Cinema and the Aula Maxima at UCC. It was in the Aula Maxima that 'Into the Twilight' by Sir Arnold Bax, the Master of the Queen's Musick, had its first performance in Ireland when it was played by Professor Aloys Fleischmann's orchestra.

My own musical education was at first confined to the piano. In my childhood there was a regrettable tendency among mothers, who otherwise in their treatment of children were above criticism, to insist on piano lessons. There was an upright piano in our house where I must have spent many hours in relentless practice, thumping out the arpeggios of Czerny. Professor Shanahan must have cringed when he saw me coming for my lesson, knowing how his piano would tremble beneath my thumps.

Fortunately, my mother had a friend in Blackrock who offered to teach me the violin. Any change of instrument was welcome and, while I never even learnt to tune the violin, I came to like Blackrock.

Blackrock was then a small fishing village where four-oared boats and a few salmon yawls anchored at the little pier beside the tram terminal. It is hard to realise how important the fishing industry was to the coastal communities of the inner harbour from Passage West up to the city. Even as late as 1930 twenty boats were fishing out of 'the Fisheries' on the Glanmire Road side of the river fronting the Oriental Bar.

Fishermen formed the backbone of the crews from Glenbrook, Monkstown, Rushbrooke and Ringaskiddy who competed at the local regattas. It was not always these crews but one of the city crews, Riverside or St Finbarr's from Frenche's Quay, who won the Blue Riband of the Lee, the Senior Pleasure-Boat class. This may seem strange but it must be remembered that the river is tidal up to a point well beyond the old city walls.

Long before the days of ships' pilots, it was these oarsmen and those from the small villages in the lower harbour who would meet incoming schooners and steer them to a berth on the quays. There was also a long tradition of rowing among the quayside dwellers and those living on Kayser's Hill, which was once a Norse settlement.

The big event of the rowing year was the race for the Leander trophy, open to senior eights. This trophy is in the form of a silver galleon and it was presented to the regatta committee in 1904. The inscription on it reads: 'This ship, freighted with gratitude and good wishes, was presented to the committee of the Cork City regatta by the Leander Club[1] as a prize to be competed for annually by eight-oared crews upon the river Lee'. The London club had won the special Senior Eights event at the Cork Exhibition of 1902, defeating the Berlin Rudder Club in a race from Lough Mahon to Tivoli.

Beyond Blackrock was Lakelands — a great stretch of meadowland where greyhounds were coursed long before Ballincollig became the venue for open coursing meetings. The fields sloped gradually to the sea, so gradually indeed that the ripples of the incoming tide came swiftly over the mud-flats to break on the pebbly shore. I often swam there with Al Murray, Eddie Spillane and a character whom we knew as 'Neptune'.

He was mahogany brown in colour from his days in the sun which, he would have us believe, had been largely spent in Arabia, though what he was doing there we never discovered. He walked with difficulty because of a hip injury, but he was completely at home in the water and had once swum from Fountainstown to Fennell's Bay.

I was sixteen at that time and it probably marked the last year that I went to the seaside with my mother. Crosshaven was our

1. 'Leander is to rowing what the MCC is to cricket,' *Sunday Times*

favourite place and my mother recalled having spent her holidays as a child at O'Leary's on Church Bay Road. Crosshaven was then far more popular with day-trippers than it is today and crowds would often gather on the cliffs near what was then Fort Camden to watch the great transatlantic liners coming in to anchor in the bay.

Programme: Cork Opera House, 1924

A World of Changing Interests

There are many easily-forgotten dividing lines in each one's life. The change from the time when myself and a few friends walked long distances to the time when we cycled was 'signposted' for me, as it coincided with the change from secondary school to university. Going through an old diary, I saw that in the summer of 1931 Tony Murphy, Mick Murphy and myself walked to Macroom. We went by way of Dripsey and Carrigadrohid, by far the best way as you have the river near you. There we played handball in Masseytown with Billie Lynch, Jerome O'Neill and Frankie Healy before returning to Cork on the following day by way of Farnanes. A week later we walked to Kinsale, went over by Summercove to Charles Fort where we again played handball before walking back to Cork, a round trip of almost forty miles in the one day!

It was at Barry's Auction Rooms in Academy Street that I bought my first (and last) bicycle, second-hand, for £4. That bicycle served me well before the frame ended up as reinforcement in a wall being built by a neighbour. One of my first trips was to Youghal where at Moll Goggin's Corner a photographer with a tripod camera took pictures of me posing smilingly beside my bicycle. Alas, the photos, not altogether unexpectedly, had faded by the time I reached Cork.

Lest it be thought that as young adolescents our pursuits were solely secular, we also went to Gougane Barra, the holy shrine of St Finbarr. That visit may well have ended in excommunication, the ultimate penalty for desecrating a holy place. There were three of us, it was high summer and while we had no swimming togs we decided, as there was no penitent or pilgrim within sight, to have a swim. Scarcely had we waded into the cold lake water, than a gruff voice ordered us out. Without waiting to see whose voice it was, we hurriedly clambered out and dressed in the grateful cover of a yew tree.

While it is generally accepted that the second marriage of a parent can have a disturbing effect on children, I welcomed my mother's second marriage. I now found myself part of a family with two of the prettiest girls in the city, Kitty and Theresa Healy. Their father, Tim Healy, also enjoyed the not inconsiderable distinction in my eyes of having been one of the Cork football team which contested the All-Ireland final of 1894.

The house in Waterloo Place proved too small for the enlarged family and before the end of 1935 we moved to Buxton Villa in Sunday's Well. This had once been occupied by an old Cork family, the Callanans. We were not long there when a caller came who introduced himself as a Callanan and asked if he might see his old room. My mother showed him in and without hesitation he mounted the stairs and, as his old room was unoccupied, walked in, lifted a floor-board and took from underneath a revolver.

He explained that he had been given it as a souvenir by a British officer on the day in 1922 when the British army left Victoria Barracks. He then thanked my mother and walked out.

In that new house many things were of course different: six flights of stairs to my bedroom beneath the roof, two inside lavatories and bathrooms but oddly enough, a hot and cold shower in the yard at the rear. There was a conservatory in the front garden and a dog kennel, but no dog. My mother loved animals — at a distance.

Before moving to Buxton Villa, I don't ever remember showing an interest in newspapers and my mother's reading of the *Cork Examiner* seemed always confined to the announcements of Deaths, Marriages and Births. 'Deaths' in particular aroused her lively interest as she sought to identify the deceased, establish his or her relationship with people whom she knew, ponder over the possible cause of death and decide whether she should or should not attend the funeral.

Then a newly-founded newspaper, the *Irish Press*, began to appear in the house. Gus Healy purchased it every day and when I was able to catch a glimpse at it, I turned to two columnists, 'Green Flag' and 'Roddy the Rover'. 'Green Flag' was the

nom-de-plume of Sean Coughlan and Aodh de Blácam wrote
under the name of 'Roddy the Rover'.

When 'Roddy the Rover' offered the prize of a handball for the
best letter from a schoolboy, I entered. I won the handball and
ever after made the game my chosen pastime. In my new-found
enthusiasm, myself and some friends decided to form a club
which we named Craobh Ruadh. I still cherish a photograph of
the founder members: Bob Fitzgerald, Dan Dennehy, Tom
O'Brien and myself.

As ballplayers we were not outstandingly successful but when
the President of Ireland, Dúbhglas de hÍde, was deprived of his
patronage of the GAA for the offence of attending a 'foreign
game', we wrote offering him the presidency of Craobh Ruadh!

Handball had an immediate appeal for me and even if I still
consider hurling to be the best of all games, I deliberately turned
to a game in which I would not have to share victory (or defeat)
with anyone else. A psychologist might base a useful study on
such a choice. Was I revealing a selfish side of my character which
was to develop as the years went on? Is Sillitoe's 'Long Distance
Runner' a single-minded introvert? Are those who prefer to
match themselves in singles competition with others, whether in
tennis or squash or table-tennis, necessarily selfish?

And my choice in handball was singles, not doubles.
Whenever I was asked to make up for a doubles match, I did so
reluctantly. This tendency persisted throughout my playing days
and spilled over into other activities. When I became secretary of
a club I preferred not to call any meeting of the committee but to
act on my own initiative, not always with successful results.
Again, when a social gathering was organised to which everyone
contributed by way of song or dance, I made sure to choose a song
that no one else was likely to know so that I would not be
'drowned' in a chorus of voices!

1931 was what modern educationists would call a 'transition
year' for me. A new house, a new interest (handball) and new
friends. One of these was Michael Murphy who lived at the
bottom of Fair Hill and we had formed the habit of going for a
'scove' together whenever we were free. (Shane Bullock makes
use of the word 'scove' when describing his schooldays at
Wilson's Hospital in Westmeath but other than that I have never
heard it used outside of Cork.)

I never knew anyone to equal Murphy as a walker. He had both style and stamina and on the hill roads beyond Nash's Boreen he was as familiar a figure as any follower of the Northern Harriers. It was bowl-playing country and many scores began from the pump outside Con Buckley's at the top of the hill. Timmy Delaney was the champion bowl player at the time but he had close rivals in 'Red' Crowley from Clancool, 'Tiger' Aherne from Pouladuff and Bill Bennett of Killeady.

A cousin of mine, James Cadden, became involved in a libel action which centred on the feats of local bowl players. He was the lessee of the licensed premises on the South Main Street known as 'The Lighthouse' and was for a time secretary of the Bowl playing Association. He was plaintiff in an action for damages against Bill Bennett and the *Southern Star* newspaper, Skibbereen.

Much of the evidence concerned the 120-foot high railway bridge on the Cork/Bandon road, known as the Chetwynd Viaduct. To loft an iron bowl over the bridge would seem to be impossible and this was the opinion of Cadden. Bennett contended that he had done it in 1902 with a 28oz bowl. Older men than either of them believed that Buck McGrath and Owen Egan had each lofted the bridge. Trial Judge O'Donnell expressed surprise that the matter was ever brought before the court and said so, before giving judgement against my relative. (Many years later, in 1955, the great Mick Barry of Waterfall lofted a 16oz bowl over the bridge and in 1977, when the railway line had long been closed, Denis Scully of Cork and Arnold Domeyer of Germany each succeeded in clearing the bridge with their throws.)

To shorten the road on a long walk there is nothing to equal a pair of bowls. This was especially true in the past when country roads were not tarred and when there was little or no traffic. One of our favourite walks was to Blarney and then north to Courtbrack or Monard. The Templemichael shovel mills were owned by the Porteous family and, as we knew Matty Porteous, we often called there. His workforce was never large but in the 'thirties dozens of different spades and turf-cutting slanes were being manufactured in that tiny village beside the Blarney river.

When it was my turn to choose a route for a day's walk, we usually turned towards the west along the Lee Road. Just where the road begins, beneath the shadow of Shanakiel, lived Sir John Harley who, as High Sheriff of Cork, wrote to King George V in 1920 seeking the release of Terence MacSwiney. In his reply, the

King's Secretary, Lord Stamfordham, explained that 'the case of the release of the Lord Mayor of Cork is one in which the King's clemency can only be exercised by His Majesty as so advised by his responsible Ministers'.

A few hundred yards farther on is 'Lacaduv', built in 1909 by M.J. Horgan as a wedding present for his son, John J. Horgan, a very able solicitor with an extensive law practice in the city and generally referred to locally as 'Quotation John'. He was Coroner for South-East Cork in 1915 when the verdict of the jury on the victims of the 'Lusitania' was 'wilful and wholesale murder' against the Emperor and Government of Germany. This verdict the *Times* described as 'one of the most remarkable the world has ever heard of'.

We rarely went past the Kerry Pike but turned down to the river by 'Ardnalee', home of Frank Daly, the butter merchant. We crossed the Shournagh river at the Crubeen Bridge, site of one of the boundaries of the Liberties of Cork as far back as 1462. We then left the road and entered the Lee Fields opposite the Watergate Flour Mills, since demolished, at the end of the Carrigrohane Road and so, as Pepys might say, 'to home'.

If, as is said, the thoughts of youth are long, long thoughts, we had an opportunity of realising our youthful dreams during that summer of 1931. The submarine 'Nautilus' en route for the North Pole was taken in tow by the American battleship 'Wyoming' when her batteries failed while off the coast of Cork. The captain of the battleship summoned the tug 'Morsecock' to take the submarine from the outer harbour up to the city where she was moored at the Albert Quay. Sir Hubert Wilkins, the Australian-born explorer, who commanded the submarine, let it be known that he might need additional crew.

A few of us decided to write to the captain. It was a sort of joint application. We handed it to a member of the crew and then sat on the quayside awaiting a reply. Within a very short time a uniformed officer came down the gangway, thanked us for our interest and added that, regrettably, we were too young. He might have said, as far as I was concerned, that 'mercifully' we were too young. What would I have done away from my mother, miles under the sea, with sharks and other monsters of the deep looking in at me!

My mother's second marriage lasted only five years and when it ended she, together with my sister and myself, moved house again. My mother was distressed by the emotional upset, the more so at having to go to court to claim alimony. Cork was then a smaller place than it is today and she must have been wounded in her pride by what many would have seen as a failure on her part. Happily, our new home provided her with the interest of new neighbours and an opportunity to devote more time to gardening, of which she was very fond.

Our new home was Janeville, a small terraced house in lower Sunday's Well. Sunday's Well was in many respects a microcosm of the city. On the higher slopes overlooking the river were the homes of the wealthy; as you came down from the heights you met with more modest dwellings. The fronts of the houses in Upper Sunday's Well were hidden behind anonymous walls of stone and brick, our new home was almost at river level and salmon were netted within yards of our front garden.

And it may be said with truth that many of the salmon lived dangerously. On a summer's day up to half-a-dozen men with fishing-rods might have been seen sitting on Wellington Bridge (efforts to call it by its official name, Thomas Davis Bridge, have not been entirely successful) watching their lines as they drifted with the current beneath. The casual passer-by could easily have been deceived by the pleasant scene. Disciples of Isaak Walton, he would have said to himself, endeavouring to catch the wily salmon. A closer glance would have shown him that none of the hooks were baited and that the flies which are tied with such care to lure the salmon were missing. Instead, each line carried six to eight hooks designed to impale any fish unwary enough to approach too closely.

Should a bailiff be seen, then 'snip', the lines were cut and half a dozen fishermen were to be seen sitting on the parapet of a bridge gazing abstractedly at the running water. Should a fish be hooked, or as the more knowledgeable say 'strokehauled', at the moment of the bailiff's appearance, then an accomplice on the bank who was ready with a gaff, was admonished in a loud voice to 'take de hook out of his mout'. It was highly unlikely that the hook would be found there.

A Student at University

In the autumn of 1931 I enrolled as an Arts student in University College, Cork. Fees were low, £12 a year, students were few, fewer than seven hundred, and the transition from secondary school seemed little different from that of promotion to a higher class.

I don't think that at that time the university played an important role in the life of the city. It had little to offer in the way of technological assistance to industry, and its impact on the cultural life of Cork was limited to allowing the Aula Maxima to be used for recitals and lectures.

The college roll was largely made up of male students, most of whom were taking Medicine or Arts. Engineering students were few, Law students fewer still. The Medical School enjoyed a high reputation and Yelverton Pearson, a member of an old Cork family, had acted as Honorary Surgeon in Ireland to King George V. However, by the early 'twenties the numbers taking Medicine had fallen off considerably. This was largely because of new regulations introduced by the British Medical Association, extending the course from five to six years, and also to uncertainty in the profession as to the right to practise in Great Britain.

Why I chose to do Arts is not easy to explain. Teachers were ill-paid but they were well-thought-of and that was important in the eyes of my mother. Guidance Counselling did not exist so that pupils like myself left school with but a vague idea of what a university offered. Nor was the university more forthcoming. The Annual Report of the President was markedly uninformative and it was 1943 before statistical information on the college was available in any detail.

The fact that my sister also chose to do Arts must have pleased my mother since she probably thought of us as helping one another with our studies. We never did. By the time that the first term began in October, she had gone to live on Blarney Street with an aunt and uncle whose only child had died as an infant. Henceforth we were to live almost as strangers to one another.

To Margaret, university life represented a freedom that she had never known at her boarding school in Monaghan. She might have abused it. She never did. The riches of the library, the stimulating company of new friends, the realisation that she was rapidly earning the praise of her lecturers and professors made her enjoy the years she spent there.

She gained Honours in all her examinations but felt cut off from any social life outside the university. Blarney Street is far from the university and this meant, in the absence of any bus service, a long walk morning and evening. Gradually she came to dislike Cork which to her was old and damp and inward-looking. The pervasive claustrophobic sense of middle-class life made her long to leave it.

Once she graduated, she sought and obtained a teaching-post in England. As the years went by, her visits to Ireland became increasingly infrequent and only the exchange of birthday cards and Christmas cards served to recall our happy childhood.

Most of the professors at that time were familiar public figures and they did not shirk from involving themselves in political controversy. Among the forty Sinn Féin members of the Cork Corporation were Professors Stockley and O'Rahilly who on more than one occasion defied military orders by appearing publicly on the platforms of that organisation. While O'Rahilly later severed his connection with Sinn Féin, Stockley was still speaking at Republican meetings as late as 1936. Raymond Kennedy, Senior Lecturer in Chemistry and Alaisdir MacConaill, Professor of Anatomy, were later to identify themselves with the same cause.

The President of the College, Dr P.J. Merriman, was gentle, unfailingly courteous but ineffectual, content to make anodyne speeches at conferring ceremonies and to guard the university against the infiltration of innovative ideas. One obituary referred to his 'prudent guidance' but E.R. MacLysaght, who was a member of the governing body, was more forthright. He referred to him as 'that most ineffective of presidents, adept at turning a deaf ear to awkward questions (usually mine) and gifted with a sense of humour which he manifests at the most unexpected times'.

I was fortunate that the Faculty of Arts was then staffed by some outstanding men. Women had yet to be considered seriously for professorships and I can remember but one, Mary Ryan, professor of Romance Languages. Published work, then as now, was a valuable qualification for any academic post and this may have influenced the National University in their choice of Daniel Corkery for the Chair of English Literature. Corkery had by then, 1931, an established reputation while Sean O'Faolain, his rival for the post, was but on the threshold of his career. Assistant Lecturer in the Department was Diarmuid Ó Murchadha from Ballincollig, who was later to become Professor of English in University College, Galway. His responsibility was Old and Middle English which I found paralysingly dull.

Before taking up his appointment, Corkery had been teaching in Cork city where he was living. He was a man of great kindness and great gentleness but staunch in adhering to his conviction that only by restoring the Irish language could the people attain to full nationhood. His was perhaps the most authentic voice of all those writers who, while using the English language as their medium, sought to interpret the beliefs and customs of the Irish people. His stories are of simple folk, their struggles, their temptations, their triumphs, their defeats.

He had strong and some would say outmoded views on what was of literary value to his students. Meeting me one day in Daunt's Square when I was on my way to the Carnegie Library, then in a temporary building in Tuckey Street, he asked me what book I was reading. I showed him H.V. Morton's *In the Steps of the Master* which I had enjoyed. He dismissed him with the brusque comment, 'He's only a journalist'.

Graham Greene recounts a not altogether dissimilar incident when, as a student at Balliol, he showed an essay he had written on Pitt to his tutor who 'sniffed, kicked a coal and then said "You ought to get on as a journalist, Graham," with bitter scorn'.

When I asked Frank O'Connor what he thought of Corkery's influence on the work of the writers of his time, his answer is, I think, worth quoting: 'It is rather difficult to judge the influence, if any, on one's own work, and therefore it is hard to answer your question accurately. My personal feeling is that Corkery himself had a great influence on Sean O'Faolain and myself, but his work is so limited in scope that it can hardly be said to have any influence whatever on ours. This may seem an uncharitable judgement, though not so intended, but it is the only way I could honestly answer your question. Probably you could say that he had a great influence on us merely in terms of reaction against his work, since his work is so intensely local and addressed to such a small and select audience while ours was being directed to any audience we could find.'

As a lecturer Corkery was hesitant, undogmatic but entirely sincere. His interpretations of nineteenth-century novelists, which formed the theme of the first term's lectures, were delivered in a low, husky voice which compelled close attention. He was assured of such attention at least from the double row of nuns from the La Retraite Hostel who occupied the front of the steeply-tiered lecture hall. Religious orders controlled most second-level schools for girls, so nuns with degrees and some without were assured of employment.

It was Corkery who introduced me to Robert Gibbings, writer, poet, painter, who was a familiar figure in the streets of Cork at the time. I am tall but Gibbings loomed high over me, with a great beard and a fine leonine head splendidly captured in Marshall Hutson's bronze bust exhibited at the Royal Academy in 1948.

He lived in a house beside Carrigrohane Church where his father was rector. He describes that idyllic retreat in the introduction to *The Wood Etchings of Robert Gibbings*: 'The Rectory at Carrigrohane was a "pretty" house, with plenty of lawns and creepers. A nice sweep of a drive, with meadows on either side, swung up from the road to the porch, and behind the house a flower garden framed in thick beech hedges and backed by an acre of vegetables. There was a coach-house, stabling for three horses and lots of sheds for sticks and coal and dogs and rabbits. All that was the domain of an elderly retainer, Mr George Payne. He had a cottage rent free at our gate, and for working without thought of time for six and a half days of the week, my father paid him eleven shillings over a period of many years'.

Poetry and Prose

T he 'elderly retainer' of whom Gibbings wrote was well known to me. George Payne and myself were both versifiers competing in the same market! That market was the *Cork Weekly Examiner* which paid sums ranging from a half-crown (30p) to ten shillings (50p) for poems published. Sums sufficient to keep a poet, not given to the hedonistic pleasures of life, alive at least for twenty-four hours.

George had once attained what we considered the pinnacle of artistic recognition when he had a poem published in the *Weekly Irish Independent*. This led us to flatter him by saying that as he was English-born, he might even aspire to burial in the Poets' Corner of Westminster Abbey. The most I could hope for was burial in St Finbarr's Cemetery, where at least I might expect to find congenial company among those with whom as a boy I had 'sported and played'.

It is a truism to say that it is of high importance for anyone with a product to sell to study the market. I was aware that the *Cork Examiner* sold extensively in England, especially in Kilburn, Camden Town and wherever Cork workers were employed. So it was that my poetic offerings bore such titles as 'An Exile Remembers', 'Irish Hills', 'My Home by the Lee' etc. I played the nostalgic note unashamedly, art giving way to the prospect of material gain. And if, unlike some better-known poets, I have never lived in a garret, I did on one occasion feel the force of clerical disapproval even as did Chatterton in an earlier age.

It happened thus. I sent a poem entitled 'When Twilight's Hour is Nigh' to the *Redemptorist Record* in Belfast. This was clearly a gross misjudgement on my part. Eroticism had no place in the pages of the *Redemptorist Record* and while my poem was far from being erotic, it did contain lines with echoes, or so I hoped, of

Swinburne. I quote: 'And heart to heart and lips to lips draw nearer / When twilight's hour is nigh'.

Editorial condemnation of such sentiments was swift and sharp. In a brief letter the editor wrote from Clonard Monastery, Belfast: 'Very many thanks. I am overloaded with poetry. Besides, if you saw the moral and physical evil which follows from this heart and lip to lip business, in the gloaming ... well, you would not sing about it'.

During that first term at university a news item in the *Cork Examiner* announced the forthcoming visit to Cork of 'the last of the Bards' as Eoghan Ruadh Mac an Bháird described himself. I sought out Sigerson Clifford whom we generally referred to as 'the poet' out of respect for his genuine poetic gifts; an anthology of his poetry had been published by Macmillan. We decided that a person of such distinction as Eoghan Ruadh Mac an Bháird surely was, should not be allowed to come and go unrecognised and unnoticed. With the addition of 'Goldsmith', an employee of the local Labour Exchange, who owed his pseudonym to his quite extraordinary resemblance to the author of 'The Deserted Village', we formed an *ad hoc* committee of three.

Word was conveyed to Eoghan Ruadh that we would meet him outside the Sovereign Bar in Patrick Street, our intention being to offer him a pint or even two. Mr Walsh, the owner of the bar, had obviously been impressed by photos he had seen of poets such as Yeats and told us that he was looking forward to being introduced to our friend.

As we stood beneath Mangan's Clock outside the Sovereign at the appointed hour, along came a thickly-bearded figure with tousled red hair. He was dressed like the kerns who marched with O'Neill on Kinsale some three centuries earlier. He wore a belted jerkin from which hung a hunting-horn and two tin mugs, while slung over his shoulder was a leather knapsack. Altogether he presented a somewhat dishevelled but none the less haughty appearance.

As we sat with him in the snug listening to him discoursing on the Hill of Aileach and the visions he claimed to have seen there where once the Fianna roamed, in came 'Johnny the Ballads'. He was a local character who, to our appalled ears, began to roar rather than sing 'Boom, Why does my heart go boom'. After the first few roars, our guest rose, cast a disdainful glance in the direction of Johnny, thanked us and with a clanking of tinware took his departure.

Cork never seemed to have had a literary salon such as that at Rathgar Road in Dublin presided over by George Russell (AE). Professor Stockley and his wife, Sophie, were 'at home' on most Sunday afternoons in their home 'Woodside', Tivoli, where music was dispensed with tea. I was there once with Geraldine Neeson but my memory is that it was more of a *soirée musicale* where the guests sang or played a musical instrument.

I was a member of a short-lived poetry circle which met in a disused stables at 16A Wellington Road. The Misses Sophia and Mabel Cornwall of Frankfield were probably the most distinguished members of this group, where each òne read a poem of his or her own composition. They added a touch of class to the gathering as they drove over in a tub trap from Douglas, tied the reins to the railings on the other side of the road and threw the rugs from the trap over the pony.

We could have done with the rugs as the room was unheated and lyric poetry is not known for generating heat. The boredom of the proceedings was relieved by the consumption of cocoa prepared on a gas-ring, and the owner of the premises usually brought the meeting to a close by turning off the only light at 9.30.

There is no evidence that cocoa ever inspired great poetry. The makers do, however, claim that it induces sleep which is almost precisely the same in its effect as the reading of one another's poetry.

When in later life I heard of the Oxford Chair of Poetry, I realised how well it would have suited members of our circle. There the Professor has no students, no school, no syllabus. He is not appointed but elected for five years by such MA's of the university as are able and willing to be in Oxford on election day.

I like to think that some ardent research workers of the future may yet erect that supreme monument of literary awards — a Summer School — to the effusions of those who gathered in that bleak room during the winter and spring of 1935-36.

At some stage in the late 'thirties I abandoned the role of teenage poet, turning aside from the poverty too often associated with that *métier* in order to write articles of what may very loosely be described as being of historical interest. At first I confined myself to descriptions of old ruins — the older and the more ruined the better. However, as the market seemed promising, I moved into the field of 'historical biography'.

Never excessively scrupulous about facts, I developed a regrettable tendency to move dates, places and even long-dead persons about with but slight regard for the truth. Thus, writing of John Philpot Curran, I gave him as a graveyard companion the Hon. Elizabeth Aldworth, the first woman freemason. This seemed to me eminently reasonable as in life they could be said to have been neighbours, she in Doneraile and he in Newmarket.

A week after the publication of the article in the *Cork Weekly Examiner*, the editor forwarded to me a letter from a reader in Cardiff who pointed out that far from being buried in Newmarket, Mrs Aldworth was in fact buried in St Fin Barre's Cathedral, Cork.

Worse was to follow. I branched out into cookery and in my very first article, written in autumn, devoted myself to blackberries. Alas, knowing nothing of jam-making, I decided that one oz of sugar to one lb of fruit should be quite sufficient. (Sugar cooks were on strike in Carlow and sugar was scarce!) Scarcely had my article appeared in the *Weekly Irish Independent*, than an irate reader wrote to say that the sooner that the paper's cookery 'expert' was given alternative employment, the better for the well-being of readers.

Stimulated by the reading of such books as those of H.V. Morton which bore titles beginning with the words 'In the Steps of ....' and those of John Gunther's 'Inside' series on European countries, I turned to the writing of travel articles. To each of these I gave a title which began with the words 'I visit'. Feeling confident that not too many Irish people had visited the smaller democracies of Europe, I began with San Marino and Andorra.

The fact that I had never been outside Ireland in no way inhibited me in my description of or my comments on such countries. But once again I was to find that among the readers of newspapers, there is invariably someone with nothing better to do than to write irate letters to editors.

My article entitled 'I visit Andorra', which the *Irish Independent* published, prompted one such reader to write to the editor. The writer was at pains to point out that while in the course of centuries of self-rule, Andorra may have at times allied itself with France and at other times with Spain, at no time was its geographical position in doubt. And I had moved it from the sheltering embrace of those two countries and placed it firmly in a remote corner of the Swiss Alps.

For my more serious geographical studies, I had the great good fortune to have Professor Isaac Swain for Geography and Geology. Whereas Corkery influenced his students in a manner of which they became aware only much later in life, Swain made an immediate impact. He had been appointed to the Chair in 1909 and, even after his retirement in 1944, he maintained an interest in his former students. He and his wife continued their custom of having 'At Homes' both at 'Slemish' on the Glasheen Road and at his bungalow at Weaver's Point, Crosshaven.

At that time, Art students and Engineering students shared Geology lectures and with the aid of his untiring assistant, Philpot, Swain introduced us to the wonders of the crustacea on Little Island as well as the more dramatic splendours of the Giant's Causeway in his native Antrim. Entirely appropriate was the presentation to him on his retirement of a silver hammer and chisel inscribed 'Found at Crosshaven'.

One geological excursion to Little Island was made memorable by an invitation to tea on the lawn at Ditchley where Arthur Julian, one of Cork's best-known solicitors, was then living. It was the only occasion in my life when I saw a peacock snatch a cucumber sandwich and eat it unhurriedly before stalking rather majestically away!

As a student taking Geology in my final year, I had to undertake a work study of the limestone on the left bank of the Lee estuary and of the mud flats on the right. My project proved to be of more than ordinary interest as it embraced the area chosen some years before as the site for a new Catholic church at Turner's Cross. The Chicago architect Barry Byrne, who had studied under Lloyd Wright, designed the building, and the builder was Jack Buckley of Grattan Street. The design aroused considerable interest as it marked a complete departure from the traditional form of church architecture. There were however many problems arising from the difficulty of getting a foundation on the river silt which stretches as far as Douglas and Ballinlough.

After the builder's death in tragic circumstances, the church was completed in 1931. At first it aroused more criticism than praise but it is now agreed that it is an outstanding example of twentieth century church architecture. There are no pillars or distracting ornaments with the exception of the Stations of the Cross. These were designed and executed by Egan's of Patrick Street, a firm associated with the city for over a hundred years.

I took Latin as a degree subject and as well as attending the lectures of the Professor, Hubert Treston, I also attended those given by William Porter, Lecturer in Ancient Classics. Treston was precise, astringent and rather uncommunicative while Porter was very much in the mould of the eccentric professor beloved of novelists. He was reputed to shave each side of his face on alternate days and was known to wear his gown when cycling from his home in Lehenagh to the college. That is how I remember him, books tied to the back-carrier and the long lawn-sleeves of the gown billowing over the handlebars.

His rating as an eccentric was however much below that of the first Professor of Mathematics, George Boole, who asked the registrar to have the college clocks put a quarter of an hour behind city clocks so as to enable him to begin his lectures on time!

My History professor was James Hogan, who came to the college in 1920 having served with the East Clare Brigade of the IRA during the 'Black and Tan' war. He was then the youngest person ever to have been appointed to a Chair of History in the National University of Ireland. He had written a number of articles on the philosophical origins of National Socialism and his book entitled *Could Ireland become Communist?*, published in 1923, placed him in the forefront of aggressive Catholic thought.

James Hogan always sat at an angle from his students. His handsome profile was then seen to best advantage. Despite the posture which did appear to be contrived, he was I believe the most unassuming of men.

My first impression of him was that he was unapproachable — that was, until I failed History in my First Year examination. Some days after the results had appeared, he stopped me on my way to the Lower Grounds and advised me on what texts to study before taking my repeat examination. I still have his own copy of Alison Phillips' *History of Europe* in two volumes, which he insisted on my keeping when he learnt that there was but one copy in the college library.

What I had taken to be an air of superiority was in reality a form of shyness and while he never shirked the challenge of public debate, I think that he much preferred the quiet of his book-lined study at his home on the Model Farm Road.

Professor O'Rahilly, who was then Registrar, I never liked. I found him ill-tempered and waspish. He opposed my application to be allowed to proceed to a further degree in English Literature, relying on the statute which denied such permission to graduates with only a Pass degree. He did so despite the recommendation of the Academic Council that permission be granted. He was over-ruled but I can still see him stamping his foot and pulling impatiently at a cigarette as I faced him in his office.

He could never resist entering the fray in any controversial issue involving the college. When a medical student who, like himself, had once been a candidate for the priesthood, wrote anonymously to the *Evening Echo* in the spring of 1936 criticising some aspects of the college regulations, O'Rahilly replied in its defence. The citizens were then treated to an excellent debate conducted in the columns of the newspaper, a debate in which all the honours did not lie with the professor.

Finally, O'Rahilly called on Union Quay, the detective headquarters of the city, to intervene with a view to ascertaining the identity of the writer. Detective-Inspector Moore had little difficulty in tracing the letters to Vincent Crotty, a Fourth-Year medical student. Moore extracted a promise from O'Rahilly that the student would not be 'sent down' if the letters ceased. His name was then revealed and the matter ended amicably.

While O'Rahilly is known to have been irascible, and Ezra Pound is quoted as saying that he never knew anyone worth a damn who wasn't, he was also fair-minded enough to admit of dissension from his own views. What appeared to have irritated him most in the Crotty affair was the use by the latter in all the correspondence of the words 'Republican Club, UCC'. This he felt implied that it was one of the clubs and societies recognised by the college authorities, which it was not. Again, he rightly held that any decision to remove emblems or objects associated with British rule should be left to the same authorities.

To O'Rahilly is attributed the decision to remove the statue of Queen Victoria from the roof over the Aula Maxima; it since seems to have disappeared. St Finbarr was chosen to replace the queen and Seamus Murphy's Finbarr has the distinction of being the first religious statue to be erected over any of Ireland's third-level institutions. After all, O'Rahilly was never an Imperialist and was remembered at Blackrock College, where he was a student, for having kept his hat on and for refusing to cheer, despite the instructions of the College president, when in 1900 Queen Victoria drove past on her way into Dublin. And it is of more than passing interest that it was the Sinn Féin Lord Mayor,

Shawled woman and boy in the North Main Street.

Interior of Ford Factory on the Marina, where manufacturing of tractors began in 1917.

Henry Ford in his first car.

The Lee at Inniscarra.

Blarney Castle, mentioned in the well-known song 'The Boys of Fair Hill':
Blarney Castle stands up straight,
If you ask for fish they'll give you mate . . .

A laneway in Cork, possibly Eason's Lane (now Cathedral Lane) near the North Cathedral

Fruit seller near the North Gate Bridge.

Clothes stretched across a lane.

Irish Sleeper Omnibus Service on the Grand Parade. The service ran to Dublin every day.

In 1902 an Armenian named Batmazian who had come to Ireland by way of London, first offered 'Turkish Delight' for sale. During World War I after the Turks massacred the British at Gallipoli, he was quick to protest his Armenian nationality to some Munster Fusiliers who tried to attack Cork's 'Turkish Shop'. Under the signboard which said 'Hadji Bey et CIE', the shop remained in business until 1971, when it was sold by his son.

Daly's Bridge, called after the well-known Cork butter merchant whose generosity made it possible to build it in 1927, but also known locally as the 'shaky' bridge.

Eoin O'Mahony, (1904-1970), a recognisable figure far beyond his native Cork.

Inniscarra Dam under construction (1956).

Tomás MacCurtain, who proposed his name for the post of Registrar in 1920.

On becoming President of UCC in 1943, he appeared to lack confidence in his guiding of the college. He showed himself intolerant of able colleagues and, surrounded as he was for the most part by men of lesser ability, kept interfering and thereby accelerated existing academic and personal tensions. Bringing, as he did, an uncompromising rigour to bear on deep-rooted assumptions and attitudes, he provoked intensely polarised responses. One of those who did not conceal his animosity towards O'Rahilly was Cormac Ó Cadhlaigh, Professor of Modern Irish. In his unpublished autobiography he wrote 'Nach liom-sa ba thrua gur imíos riamh ón Mainistir agus Coláiste Cholmáin d'fhágaint mar a raibh meas duine uasail orm'.

O'Rahilly's tenure of office was, however, marked by many significant developments, notably the introduction of a Diploma course in Social Studies which attracted mature students from all the Munster counties. Before his time the college was rather hostile to any involvement of the community, but largely as a result of his efforts the legend on the main entrance, 'Where Finbarr taught let Munster learn' came nearer to reality.

The senior lecturer in Education, Eoin MacSweeney, was in charge of that Department by the time in 1935 that I came to do the Higher Diploma in Education. He was amiable, easy-going and resembled the character in Gilbert and Sullivan who 'did nothing in particular, and did it very well'.

He was also inclined to be forgetful and this was to have happy consequences for me. Each Diploma student was required to do 100 hours of classroom teaching in the course of the year and this, in theory, was to be supervised.

In the month of September I went to Greenmount National School, which was run by the Presentation Brothers, with the intention of doing my classroom teaching there. The headmaster, Brother Gilbert, with what was probably a shrewd appraisal of my inexperience and inability to control a class, simply signed the form I showed him which stated 'Thomas McElligott has completed one hundred hours teaching' and dated it for May in the year following! The headmaster is long dead but I have kept his testimonial to my teaching ability. As references of that kind are invariably given for *proven* teaching ability, mine may well be the only one for unproven ability.

Looking Back on University Years

If I were asked what I got from my years at University College, Cork, I would answer 'a degree and a diploma'. No more. It offered less than a good secondary school in the way of effective teaching and there were few compensatory activities. It was in fact a very unexacting and a very unstimulating place. Nothing much was demanded of us beyond wearing a gown to lectures and in the library and ensuring that we answered roll-call at a certain number of lectures.

It is of course true that a non-residential university can never provide anything like the same community life that students enjoy where there is on-campus accommodation for at least part of the student body. The only living accommodation on the university grounds was at the Honan Hostel where some fifty students lodged in what they considered frugal comfort.

The building was once known as Berkeley Hall and had been bought in 1908 by the Franciscan Order from Tom Donovan, later to be elected Lord Mayor of Cork. The intention was to make it available to secular students as well as to intending members of the Franciscan Order. From the outset, many Franciscans were opposed to the hostel idea and they also questioned the involvement of the friars in the work of a secular university. The decision was taken to close it and it was subsequently sold to the university in 1914.

It is, I think, worthwhile turning aside for a moment from my main narrative to say a word about Tom Donovan. First of all, he bestowed the gift of a bridge on the city. It spans the river beside the university entrance and bears the inscription '1902. Bronntanas do Mhuintir Corcaighe ó Tomás Ó Donnabháin,

Fernhurst'. Tom Donovan was a familiar figure to me as a child. He lived in a big house partly hidden by trees opposite the Bon Secours Home and exercised his grey horse in the fields where we played and which bore his name.

He was elected Lord Mayor in 1908 and again in 1909 but was denied a third term by Writ of Ouster. This was a medieval procedure for the remedying of challenged appointments. A Mr Sisk had brought a motion for judgment of Ouster against him after Donovan had defeated him in the election for Lord Mayor without having reached the statutory majority. The voting had been twenty-two for Donovan and twenty-one for Sisk, with six members of the Corporation abstaining.

Donovan was compelled to resign and a notice of Mandamus signed by George V ordered the members of the Corporation to elect a Lord Mayor 'in the place and stead of the said Thomas Donovan'.

During his years of office he had indirectly helped to secure the Chair of Scholastic Philosophy in UCC for the Capuchins. He had gone to confession at the Capuchin Friary of the Holy Trinity, as was the custom in Cork for anyone with an understanding of the way in which penance may vary from church to church and confessor to confessor. The Priest, recognising the Lord Mayor, 'nobbled' him, if the expression is permitted, to vote for the Capuchin who that day was a candidate for the Chair of Scholastic Philosophy in the university.

The meeting of the Governing Body of the university had begun when Donovan arrived at the Council chamber and he met the three Protestant members on their way out. They had decided that they ought not to vote in an election when there were but two candidates, a Dominican and a Capuchin. The Lord Mayor persuaded them to return and vote for the Capuchin. They did so and to this day the Chair is held by a Capuchin.

The main entrance to UCC leads under an archway opening on to a delightful view of the three-sided quadrangle with, in the distance, a sloping cmbankment. As I remember the campus, there was about it an air of what might have been called rural calm. It was without life and I cannot recall any turbulence, any ripple of student unrest, to disturb that calm.

To relieve the boredom of lectures, some of the female students brought their knitting, while on the bench most remote from the rostrum, Gordon Hurley — later to become a District Justice —

co-operated with me in the exacting task of filling in football
coupons.

The industry of the students occasioned the wrath of Cormac
Ó Cadhlaigh who, addressing himself as it appeared to no one in
particular, announced '*Ní cheadófar d'éinne maisín fuaghála no
cniotála do thabairt isteach sa seomra seo*'. Cormac, who was an able
and forceful lecturer, was later to show his gifts as a salesman and
I attended a lecture of his at UCD, when, holding up a copy of
Gnás na Gaeilge, he recommended it to the class, saying '*B'fhiú
díobh an leabhar seo do léamh. Sár-leabhar's ea é agus togha Gaeilge ann.
Slad-mhargadh é ar cheithre scillinge*'.

Some of the rigidity of the secondary school system carried
over to the college and there was no interaction between student
life and that of the people 'down town'. When the last lecture of
the day had been delivered, rarely later than five o'clock, to all
intents and purposes the college closed down. Future doctors,
teachers, engineers and lawyers went their separate ways.

Only on such occasions as Rag Day did they fraternise. Few
who recall those days will forget Tomás MacCurtain
masquerading as Mae West. He sailed rather than walked
through Patrick Street, wearing an amazing widebrimmed
flowered hat, pirouetting and curvetting under a brilliantly
coloured parasol. They will remember also the irrepressible Joe
Kerrigan who allowed himself to be bound and thrown into the
Lee at Patrick's Bridge before being rescued by Bat O'Driscoll of
Bandon and his leopard-clad warriors. The day always ended
with Bill Twomey and Noel Dalton dressed as negro minstrels
playing outside the old Tivoli Restaurant.

If I were asked to say what is the main difference between
student life in the 'thirties and that of today, I would suggest that
there was then an almost complete absence of stress. This was due
in large measure to the fact that failure in examinations, no matter
how frequent, did not entail rustication. A few 'ancients' were
always to be found sitting on a few fatigued chairs in 'the Rest'
who, so it was said, had been at the college since the First World
War.

They were wont to bestir themselves only to go as far as 'Starry
Murphy's' on the Western Road, there to discuss such serious
matters as how to 'crash' the Saturday night dance at the Arcadia
or where to pawn the landlady's furniture while she was away.

Alas for those who may argue that the presence of such

venerable students lent a touch of *'je ne sais quoi'* to the college, a statute was passed in 1946 whereby any student who failed four examinations was 'out'.

Reading of life at Oxford and Cambridge during the same years presents a picture that had no parallel in my experience at UCC. It may have been that the Cork college was then too small and had not had time to develop distinctive customs and traditions. Time was needed for the colleges to adjust to the political changes that had taken place in the decade following the foundation of the National University.

Much energy in the post-Treaty years went into the task of transmitting our cultural heritage and the preservation of the language. The nationalism of the time as expressed by some of the more ardent language enthusiasts was both intolerant and exclusive. It was the nationalism of a beleaguered people who for long had fought against external forces and were finding it difficult to accommodate to new thinking on old loyalties.

This bred a spirit of conservatism even among the young who turned aside from the equally necessary task of confronting changes in society. I found myself taken aback some years later when, as a teacher, I first stood in front of a class of teenagers. Where was the timidity with which we, even as undergraduates, ventured a muted criticism of our professors ? Where was the regard for the intellectual judgments of their elders?

In a university with but one college on the campus, there was never any need for cohesiveness in the face of other pressures. The only occasion when UCC seemed aware of its separate identity was when matches were played against other universities. The competitions for the Dudley Cup (rugby), the Fitzgibbon Cup (hurling), the Ashbourne Cup (camogie), the Sigerson Cup (football) and the Chilean Cup (hockey) were all focal points for demonstrations of noisy loyalty.

Life outside the college walls never seemed to touch us and while the Blueshirt movement roused some momentary interest in politics, that quickly subsided. Cork city and county had been the scene of clashes with the police in the course of which a man was shot dead in Anglesea Street, yet I can remember but one student being imprisoned, and that only briefly, for his activities as a Blueshirt. Alone of the college societies, the meetings of the Literary and Philosophical Society on a Saturday night provided evidence of the animated discussions that students are believed to delight in.

It was a President of UCC who made the most damning comment on the insularity that seemed to have been accepted by students and faculty alike, when he said 'what we must guard against is the infiltration of ideas into the university'. It was therefore a cause of no great surprise when a motion, 'That this House deprecates the intrusion of Ecclesiastical Authorities in political matters' was taken off the noticeboard by order of the President and the meeting of the 'Phil' on 2 February 1935, at which it was to have been debated, was banned.

Louis Marcus tells of the chilling reception accorded to a one-act play of his by the then President Harry Atkins who, having read it, made it clear that if Marcus were a Catholic he would have been expelled.

Not until long after my time at UCC was a pamphlet issued which drew attention to the need for a more combative self-assertiveness on the part of the students. That was in 1958 when three graduates, John Horgan, John O'Shea and Donall Farmer, published *The Conveyor Belt*. In it they refer to the incivility of the President's office staff and went on to castigate student unconcern:

'Students at the university are culpable principally of irresponsibility of action, and also of apathy. One half of them assumes pretensions of being "different", and includes the duffers and those with amazingly developed views on literary criticism, as well as those religious sophists who, though professing anticlericalism, haven't the guts to practise it. The other and far more likeable half includes those who exert themselves at push-penny in the Men's Club, and who show no sign of advancing beyond a stage of mental development common to most Primary Certificate candidates'.

I can recall but one occasion when students of the university ventured even a mild protest. It concerned incidents taking place many miles from UCC, but which did affect two of its graduates.

In May 1933 Dr Finbar Quinlan was appointed medical officer for the Loughrea Dispensary in County Galway at a salary fixed at £500 a year. The Appointments Commission had considered the application of two other doctors before recommending that Dr Quinlan, whose address was given as Inse Geimhleach, be appointed.

He and his wife, Eileen O'Driscoll, an Arts graduate of the

university, were soon made aware that his appointment was resented by the townspeople who favoured the son of the previous doctor. Stones were thrown at the house they occupied, windows in his car were broken, his wife was threatened with assault and eighty to one hundred Gardai had to be drafted into the town on dispensary days.

The medical students voiced their protest at a meeting held on the steps of the city jail where Professor Stockley and Dick Anthony, TD, joined them. They associated themselves with the protest in order to assert the right of an Irishman to practise his profession or work at his trade in his own country.

In the autumn of 1942, long after the tumult had died down and some of the assailants been jailed, a play by Elizabeth Connor, entitled 'An Apple a Day', based on the Loughrea incidents, was produced at the Abbey Theatre.

My own contribution to college life was slight. I did go to meetings of *An Chuallacht* and later of the *Comhchaidreamh* and turned out fairly regularly for hurling practice at the Mardyke. And there, one Sunday afternoon when no student who wasn't disabled or under suspension for such crimes as attending foreign dances could be found, I was pressed into service as goalkeeper on the senior team. In front of me at full-back was the redoubtable Dick Molloy but even he could not repel all the opposing forwards. The *Cork Examiner's* report of the match stated that 'the College goalkeeper was replaced midway through the first half'. That effectively ended my career as a hurler.

Reductions were made on admission charges to certain places such as cinemas and dance-halls on production of a student card. I availed of this concession to visit the Cork Turkish Baths. I may have been the only student ever to do so! What struck me at once was the curtain of warm air that met me on walking in off the South Mall. The baths themselves were something of a disappointment. I had expected a great hall with onion domes and minarets where soft-sandalled attendants proffered long hookahs as one lay in the tepidarium. Instead, I found myself being kneaded and pummelled by Jerome Twomey from Blarney Street who did not even wear a turban. As I walked out into the cold of a winter's night, I took comfort from an inscription in the hallway which stated that 'without ablution prayer will be of no value in the eyes of God'.

It could with truth be said that in the year 1936, by which time

I had spent five years at the college, I had made no contribution of any sort — academic or social — to the life of that institution. Finding myself in my final year taking Geography with but five other students, all girls, I decided to speak to none of them. Not to do so required stern discipline on my part, as the laboratory work involved the study of rock samples and the sharing of microscopes for the examination of slides.

Psychiatrists might have defined my behaviour as a negative affirmation of personality. Whatever it was, it did much to establish my reputation as an eccentric.

Eccentricity takes myriad forms. I was someone who had never studied in the college library or borrowed a book therefrom, who had never attended a college 'Hop' whether in the Gresham Rooms in Maylor Street or in the St Francis Hall in Sheares Street, who had never entered the college restaurant and never 'dated' a college girl.

At a time when money was scarce in a way that the present generation must have difficulty in understanding, a date with a girl meant going for a walk and, only very infrequently, going to the cinema. And just as there were certain recognised trysting places such as Singer's Corner, Mangan's Clock, the 'Col' Corner, so there were certain roads considered to be more favourable to romance than others. The Black Ash beyond Turner's Cross, Lover's Walk in Tivoli and Tory Top Lane in Blackrock were then sufficiently remote to be beyond parental vision.

With but a sketchy sex education, casually acquired through the family or transmitted by pals, most of the young men among whom I grew up shied away from any affairs that might have led towards the altar. In many cases there were sound economic reasons for non-involvement but it was Catholic teaching that left most of us even later in life feeling ill-at-ease and unprepared when faced with the idea of marriage.

There was then no 'café life' such as young people now enjoy and only when I was in my twenties and working did I venture into the Pavilion or the Savoy. A few of us who played handball used to meet afterwards in Buckley's of Marlboro Street where a pint of milk and a doughnut cost sixpence. Single-sex activities encouraged a single-sex social life.

The 'thirties was not the most liberal of decades for adolescents. In the country 'platform dances' at crossroads became the victim of clerical opposition which had as one of its effects the building of unsightly and unhygienic 'ballrooms of romance'. In Cork city vigilantes under the banner of St Jude tarred the elm trees on the Mardyke and saw to it that 'unsuitable' books were removed from bookshops.

Both boys and girls accommodated themselves easily to the reality of a situation in which flirting was accepted as a practical substitute for more formal introductions. In a compact city such as Cork, casual relationships which were established as a result of 'pick-ups' had no effect on the morals of the community. On the basis of the saying that a good fox never kills near home, my friends and myself were inclined to favour out-of-town dance halls when in search of female companionship. We went through a period when only Ceilidhes and Old-Time Waltzes would satisfy our cultural aspirations, but the realisation that the really sophisticated girls were more likely to be found doing the fox-trot and tango brought us back to the city.

The dance-halls did no more than romanticise our idea of women: the sexual aspects were as yet unclear rather than unknown to us. We did, like everyone else in Cork, 'scuttle' off down to the Holy Trinity Church whenever we had sinned against the sixth Commandment. Not that the commandment was exactly informative but our ignorance led us to believe that only Father John, OFM Cap., could deal with any deviation from the strict orthodoxy laid down by those five words 'Thou shalt not commit adultery'.

Despite turning my back on the college in so many ways, it had earned a place in my affections by the time I left it or, rather, I had begun to see it as a link between different stages of my life.

I was a very small child when the first college bridge over the south channel of the Lee was swept away in the floods of 1917. I was brought there in 1922 when my aunt Mary, a nun in the Order of St Louis, was doing a Summer Course under the auspices of the Celtic Faculty. It was there that I saw my first Shakespearian play, *A Midsummer Night's Dream*, on the sloping embankment on the south side of the quadrangle — a perfect stage for that light-hearted play. And in the Lower Grounds beside the lake, I once found a mallard's nest hidden in the bamboo canes beside the water's edge.

Today, when I watch hundreds of students streaming over the bridge now linking different parts of the Science Block, Memory, at my bidding, replaces them with those who idled and laughed with me, 'Drifted about along the streets and walks, /Read lazily in trivial books'.

During that summer of 1936 I became aware that there was no clamant demand for my services as a teacher. Preparations for war had not yet affected the supply of teachers in England, while at home almost two-thirds of all secondary teachers were in religious orders. Fortunately, there were grinds. The word 'grind' must be one of the least euphonious in the English language but it does convey something of the drudgery associated with what I have come to consider an unprofessional activity. Let me add that to ensure survival, I took part in that 'unprofessional activity'.

Grinds were most frequently called for in Irish. The Appointments Commission was insistent that for all public offices some acquaintance with the language was necessary. I gave grinds to mental hospital attendants, to poultry instructresses, to employees of the Dairy Disposals Board, to warble-fly inspectors, to School Attendance Officers, and for all this mental slavery which, had I continued, would almost certainly have destroyed all my brain cells, I charged a half-crown (thirty pence) an hour!

One thing that the experience led me to believe was that the teaching of Irish was abysmally bad largely because the grammarians had ignored the spoken tongue and imposed their will upon the teachers to do so.

Generally speaking, university students did not then work during the summer vacation. Their efforts to avoid it during term were considered to have rendered them unfit for anything but complete rest. I broke with that tradition in the summer of 1932 when I was employed for some weeks by the firm of Johnson and Perrott. This firm had resulted from a 'marriage' dating back to 1810 between James Johnson who manufactured landaus and broughams in what was then Nelson Place, and Richard Perrott of the Hive Iron Works in Washington Street. The carriage trade had declined by the time of my brief association with the firm but I do remember handing out brochures at the stand which the firm had at the Cork Summer Show. Vauxhall cars and Bedford trucks were some of 'our' main lines. I could have sold you a Vauxhall Cadet for £345 but Fordson trucks would have cost you a good deal more, though they did have some delightful accessories such as demountable rims, pneumatic tyres and electric lighting.

During that summer my favourite haunt was the weir on the

river Lee just where it begins to divide itself in two. As I lived nearby I reached the weir through a gate marked 'Private', confident that Mr O'Riordan, the Waterworks Resident Engineer, would not invoke the powers that were his to bar my entry.

I could then either lie on the weir itself if the river was not in flood or cross over to the Lee Fields and enjoy the conversation of those who had come out from the city. Many of these were 'regulars' dedicated to the twin joys of inertia and inaction. They lay on a stretch of desiccated grass beside the old open-air baths, prepared to discourse on a wide range of topics.

The French have a word for those who engage in no work involving undue physical effort but who prefer the more civilised pursuit of constructively wasting time! A person who savours the beauties of town or country, observing people and places out of sheer curiosity, who learns something of life from life itself, is known as a *flaneur*.

These Leeside *flaneurs* could have been snagging turnips, earthing potatoes or singling carrots in the market gardens at Inchigaggin but they showed a clear preference for matters of the mind. Most if not all lived outside the conventions imposed by education and ambition. For them the race was not to the swift but rather a serenity that was achieved without any excessive and purposeless effort. Only when the sun in its diurnal course left them temporarily in the shadow did they disturb themselves.

Like the Sun King of an earlier age, these men held court, dispensed counsel and gave judgement on matters of the day. And if the setting was less splendid than Versailles, they had the shining river beside them in which to mirror their thoughts.

When discussing such abstract subjects as work, the less inactive did have some vague ideas of writing and some even went so far as to submit articles to *The Leeside Lyre* and *The Mistletoe*, each of which was published by the Leeside Press. For the most part, they looked on literature as something associated with leisure and they never considered it as a means of earning a living.

At intervals during the day one of them would bestir himself and tumble rather than dive into the river. Such unnatural displays of energy were not looked upon with favour by the other 'balmers' for whom breathing was the only sustained effort of which they were capable. It was not until the westering sun and a chill in the air told them of the coming on of evening that they stood up, shook themselves like swans about to take flight, discarded bathtowels bearing such legends as 'Birmingham Corporation Baths', 'Property of Blackpool Baths', etc and returned to the city.

Before the end of that summer I got an unexpected day's work when a call came from Fred Barter, Messrs Cook's agent in Cork, for thirty student guides to accompany French tourists on their one-day coach tour of counties Cork and Kerry.

With one or two exceptions, none of us spoke a single word of French but a crash course given by Jim Buckley from the Western Road provided each of us with what was considered to be the indispensable minimum for a qualified guide, namely four words. When the tourists came ashore at Glengarriff from the cruise liner 'Lafayette' on that July morning in 1936, I stood beside my coach calling out *'Deux, s'il vous plait'*. The numeral indicated to which of the thirty coaches they were assigned.

The tour embraced the Pass of Keimaneagh, Gougane Barra, Macroom and Killarney. They enjoyed their day. So did we except for their insistence on being shown shamrock, that most elusive and virtually unobtainable trefoil on the island of Ireland.

Sport in the City

By the mid-thirties I was twenty-one which is, I suppose, a milestone of some sort in the life of everyone. I was confident that a teaching post would one day come my way and meanwhile I enjoyed handball, hurling and hiking.

The folk-heroes of my earlier years, who were almost all hurlers, were now giving way to sports stars in a variety of sports. Rugby had a struggle to exist at all and as my home was only the breadth of the river from the Mardyke Grounds, I could count the hundred or so who attended the matches there on Saturday afternoons. The game suffered from the elitist tag and it was the newer clubs like Sunday's Well and Highfield who helped to broaden its appeal.

Soccer had lost much support with the departure of the British Army in 1922 but many ex-soldiers continued to live near what had been Victoria Barracks. They formed the Barrackton Soccer Club and drew support from the nearby streets and squares, which had been, in the words of Frank O'Connor, 'deserted by God and the Cork Corporation'.

The club was on one occasion playing St Vincent's in a Munster League match at the Camp Field. Their opponents were from the strongly Republican Blarney Street. Barrackton were winning easily and looked like taking both points when a shot rang out. A St Vincent's supporter had simply drawn a revolver and shot the ball!

My own interest in handball led me to the Old Market Place, a cobbled square with a few gaunt tenements flanking the licensed premises then owned by Tim Horgan and which proclaimed itself in letters of gold to be 'the Cork City Ballcourt'. There I passed many sunlit days on the front steps waiting for a game of handball while across the way Shandon ticked away the hours from eternity and, more importantly for us, the hours that separated us from dinner or tea.

The bar was a 'tied house' meaning that it was leased to the licensee by Murphy's Brewery, which at one time owned more than seventy public houses in the city. Over one hundred years ago, it was described as an ale-house when an application was made by the Company for the transfer of the licence from Patrick Twomey, the then owner. The Company sold their interest in the premises in 1976.

The ballcourt was situated at the rear, surrounded or so it seemed by slaughter-houses, bearing out the words of Lord Ossory who a century earlier was quoted as saying that Cork was 'the slaughterhouse of Ireland, full of butchers, hogs and pigs'. When I came to know the ballcourt, all of seventy years ago, the great supporters of the game who did not hesitate to gamble ten or twenty sovereigns on a rubber were all butchers — Dillons, Looneys, Nevilles and Coughlans.

American players were regular visitors, coming to compete in the Cork Tournament, the classic event of the handball season. On such occasions the gallery might include such local celebrities as W.F. O'Connor, State Solicitor; Alderman Dick Anthony; J.J. Hayes of the Grand Hotel, Crosshaven; J.J. Walsh, later to be Minister for Posts and Telegraphs; Joe Donnelly, the baker; Jimmy Donnelly, the bookmaker; and 'Mikus' Creedon, the boxer.

'Classic events' were not for me and until I acquired some skill, I played in the three-wall court behind the Model School in Anglesea Street or in the gloomy covered court attached to the Presentation Monastery at Greenmount. The rubber ball or 'cock standard' which we used was marketed by Elvery's of Patrick Street and there I first met Mr Deasy who spent fifty-eight years with the firm and who greeted everyone with a smile and the words, 'Well, friend'.

On Sunday mornings I went up to the North Monastery where Brother O'Brien and his partner, Brother Gregg, were almost unbeatable in a ballcourt which held such hazards as netted windows, down pipes and unfinished right-hand wall. My partner in many a rubber was Frank Brady, the former soccer international, who had begun his career with Fordsons.

I decided that the game needed more competition than that provided by the GAA, which looked on handball as the poorest of poor relations whose demise would have been welcomed by them. Canon Hamilton, Chairman of the Clare County Board (GAA), used to say that ballplayers gambled and Canon Punch, Chairman of the Limerick Board held that ballplayers drank. While I had good reason to know that both judgements were correct, I felt that their remarks could have been extended to include hurlers and footballers.

Be that as it may, I decided to run a tournament for handballers. Entries came from a very wide range of players some of whom could be described as ballplayers only by a generous interpretation of the word. A faded sheet lies before me as I type, giving the 1st Round draw:

A. Murphy	v	A. Kelly;
R. Fitzgerald	v	W. Rea,
T. Dennehy	v	M. Coppinger,
I. Ross	v	A. Murray,
P. Herlihy	v	T. Buckley,
M. Murphy	v	J. O'Mahony,
D. Twohig	v	J. Lenihan,
T. Ryan	v	P. Slattery,
J. Hogan	v	M. Herlihy,
J. Morley	v	E. Carroll,
D. Hawkins	v	B. Whelan,

T. McElligott a bye.

Each paid one shilling (twelve pence); winner to take all. Some rather sharp observations were made on the good fortune of the recipient of the bye but far sharper were the remarks when the same 'recipient' won the prize of twenty-three shillings.

While I was then long left the Lough parish, I still followed the fortunes of the St Finbarr's hurling team. I had seen them playing at Wilton in an open field stretching down from the old brick house of the Leslie family. I had followed them from Greenmount to Togher, I had watched them meeting at Phair's Corner at the foot of the Lough Road, I had worn their blue colours when they won and when they lost.

Even in the 'thirties when his glory days were over, I can remember stopping to look in wide-eyed admiration at 'Dannix' Ring when I saw him one day working with, I think, the Cork Gas Company, on Wyse's Hill. 'Dannix', one of the most stylish of all midfield hurlers for St Finbarr's, Cork, and Ireland.

On the day of a county final involving St Finbarr's, I could be sure to see such well-known supporters as Squash, Din-Din, Cola,

Chawky, Tear-Drop, Count, Bag O'Nails, Dirty Collar, Chateye, Yellow Dinny, Down-Down, Papal Guard, Style O'Man, Bacchus and many others whose real names were unknown to me, making their way along the touchline at 'the Park'. One follower who rejoiced in the title of 'the Commodore' owed this to the fact that he had introduced model-yachting to the Lough!

As I never had the price of admission, I watched many matches on the Mardyke from the railings surrounding the grounds. While the railings were far distant from the actual playing pitch, this did not prevent advice, threats and abuse being heaped on players and referees. I saw at least one hockey international, Ireland v Wales in 1933, and one soccer international, Ireland v Hungary in 1939, from the vantage point of the railings before the grounds were altered and we, the non-paying public, were denied our 'free entertainment'.

On the days of big matches a blind man known as Blind Peter was to be seen sitting on a stool at the entrance to the 'Dyke opposite 'Starry' Murphy's public house. There, in a voice hoarse from rough usage in all weathers, he cried unceasingly, 'Help the blind and may God spare your eyesight and protect you from sickness, danger and death'.

Throughout 1935 and most of 1936 I was, statistically speaking, an 'unemployed graduate'. If that definition could have been further refined, I was a 'contented unemployed graduate'. And with twenty-four hours to enjoy in each day, I saw many sides of life in the city.

The 'thirties was a time of considerable activity in boxing and wrestling and I often made my way to the gym in Maylor Street where local boxers with such intimidating names as 'Butcher' Howell and 'Cyclone' Murray were to be seen skipping, punching, shadow-boxing and, as is the way with all boxers, grunting. Trainers, mostly stout and bald-headed, flapped towels, sponged heads and generally urged their charges to further violence.

I had a pal, Paddy Roche, who trained there and who, after winning the Irish welterweight title, turned professional and went to London. There he was known as 'Sketchy' and he became extremely popular with the patrons of the Devonshire Club in Holborn and also at The Ring in Blackfriars. It was the custom at Blackfriars to throw money in the ring at the end of a contest if the boxers had given good value. On one occasion in 1937 Paddy and his opponent shared £8 10s ¼d — a sum which was taken to indicate great satisfaction.

The two most colourful personalities to visit that gym, though I do not remember that either of them trained there, were Jack Doyle and Danno Mahony. Jack was our idol. As a boy he had worked on coal boats and on the tenders servicing Atlantic liners in his native Cobh. He became a professional boxer, won fights and lost fights. The result did not seem to matter. Jack was the boxer who made a triumph of failure.

He attracted the crowds and even when he lost and his victorious opponent had left the ring, it was Jack who was cheered. It was his autograph that was sought. He lost to Petersen, he lost to Robinson, he lost to Phillips. Their arms were raised in victory but the cameras and the flash-bulbs focused on Jack as, wrapped in a green silk dressing gown, he led the crowd in singing 'Mother Machree'.

When at some stage of his career he appeared at the Opera House with Fred Curran and his Dancing Girls, he was billed as 'world champion'. He was then married to Judith Allen and the show was known locally as 'the Punch and Judy' show. No indication was given or indeed looked for by his adoring fans as to the sport in which he was world champion. It cannot have been for boxing but then a certain extravagance is permitted in what is, after all, part of show business. My own handball partner, Christy Kelly from Cat Lane, boxed professionally as 'Kid Kelly from the Fiji Islands' though he had scarcely ever been farther than Little Island.

Facing the Atlantic in the town where Jack was born is a small rectangle of grass. At one end is a plaque to John F. Kennedy, at the other end a plaque to Jack Doyle. Each awakens different memories for the passer-by.

Both Doyle and Danno Mahony had made their debut in the world of sport while serving as soldiers, Doyle with the Irish Guards and Danno in the Irish Army. Doyle had been bought out but the discovery of Danno was quite accidental.

A car driven by Father Cashman, the Catholic curate in Ballydehob, had skidded off the road during frosty weather. He was uninjured and he looked about him for help. Danno, on weekend leave from the Curragh, happened to be walking down the hill from his home in Dereenlomane. Father Cashman asked him to get a pair of traces and a horse to pull the car out of the dyke. By way of answer, Danno simply gripped the rear bumper and lifted out the car.

Father Cashman spoke to him and found that his two-year short service contract in the army was almost at an end. On his discharge Cashman recommended him to a professional trainer in Cork city and so began the career which led to his winning the world's professional wrestling title.

Danno's brothers, Florrie in particular, had excelled at throwing the 56lb weight at local sports meetings while his father, when no longer young, had been known at a fair day in Ballydehob to leap into a creel in order to examine some bonhams brought in for sale.

My own association with the 'Grunt and Groan' game dated from 1936 when Gerald Egan, a sports promoter, staged a number of spectacular wrestling contests in Long's Field at Victoria Cross. In one of these Danno was billed to wrestle Charlie Strack, an 18-stone American. Stewards were needed and I was taken on, given a badge, a blackthorn stick and a promise of fifteen shillings.

As a steward I was not a success. A steward at an open-air wrestling contest in Ireland needs qualities in which I was lacking. He needs to be able to hold back the sway and surge of hundreds of large men, each one of whom is determined to pay no entrance charge, to sit at the ringside and, if provoked, to inflict physical damage on anyone near him. When I saw the crowds pushing aside such frail obstacles as wrought-iron gates and barbed-wire fences and when I realised that they were prepared to trample on much-loved grandmothers to reach the ringside, I decided to resign my stewardship. This I did by putting my badge in my pocket and placing my blackthorn under a seat.

Relieved of my responsibilities, I proceeded to enjoy the spectacle of Danno's attempts to dismember Strack. At one stage of the contest the latter was seated on Danno's back, occupied apparently in methodically gouging out his eyes. Such cruelty, even in wrestling, was thought to be excessive and after the referee had sought in vain to separate them, Danno with a mighty heave displaced Strack and in the best tradition of a thriller film, with one bound was free. He then began to swing Strack round and round before slamming him not once but many times face downwards on the mat.

Sensing that the end was near, one ex-steward made his way

quietly to the exit, pausing only to collect fifteen shillings at the box-office.

We tend to think that in distant days the sun shone more brightly, autumn days were more golden and winters more sharp. The summer of 1936 was the last I was to spend in Cork before taking up work as a teacher, though of course I was often to return, and I look back on it as golden.

It was a time when I had little or no money. My mother and I lived frugally but very happily and when in later life I regretted not having had money to afford my mother more of the pleasures of life, I was reminded that where others enjoyed spending, she enjoyed saving. Her only income was from the alimony which she received each month and some dividends from shares in the Cork Gas Company and the GSR.

I inherited some of her habits and rather than spend the money of the Cork Handball Committee, of which I was secretary, on stamps, I delivered most letters by hand. That meant that when I organised an inter-firm tournament, I walked out to Sunbeam-Wolsey in Blackpool, to Ideal-Weatherproofs in Glanmire and to Dunlops on the Marina as well as to firms with offices within the city.

A hole in the hedge between our house and that of my mother's nearest neighbour, Mrs O'Sullivan, ensured that in the morning Mrs O' Sullivan's *Cork Examiner* was read by each in turn, and in the evening my mother's *Evening Echo*. They were good friends yet neither ever visited the other's house!

My own contribution to 'good neighbourliness' was to trim the hedges of all five gardens in the terrace.

Two or three times a week I would cycle the five miles to Ballincollig with Brother Urban of the South Monastery or Father O'Flynn of the Augustinians. The small ballcourt, fifty-five feet by twenty-eight, was ideal for singles. The barracks had remained unoccupied after the departure of the British and not until 'the Emergency' did it again echo to the sound of marching men.

We played the best two out of three games or, if we were energetic, three out of five. Not infrequently, as the result of a dispute over the score, we cycled back to the city in silence!

Sometimes when I tired of handball, I would call across the river and ask the groundsman, Larry O'Shea, to leave a side-gate open and then a few of us would go and play hurling. It was all so carefree, so haphazardly so. Ever since then I am inclined to blame 'the Emergency' for changing our habits. Men in uniform, drill, parades, shouted commands — is it all a bit foreign to the Celtic temperament?

Few of my friends had togs, fewer still equipment of any sort. Admittedly, we were not part of the tennis circuit nor did we ever aspire to play cricket for Cork County, yet we never thought of these sports as being 'exclusive'. They were less widely played, that was all.

We knew, and of course boasted, that Cork had the best golfer in Jimmy Bruen, the best tennis-player in Harry Cronin, the best cricketer in N.C. Mahony, the best yachtsman in Harry Donegan, the best swimmer in Bill Noonan, and the best rugby player in Jack Russell. And if some of these excelled in what some Christian Brothers were known to describe as '*Cluichí na hImpireachta*', so be it. Each of them was 'one of our own'.

When awards have been awarded and prizes presented, there remains one player in the Cork of my youth who, even if he had never won a medal, had no equal as an all-rounder. Whether down at the Showgrounds playing for Cork Bohem- ians, or on Glasheen Road where he turned out for Harlequins or on the Mardyke with Dolphin, Brian Curtis was always in demand and always ready to play. Yet it was not on land but in water that he was at his best. Whether the event was back-stroke, side-stroke or breast-stroke, Brian was to be seen surging through the water to win or lose with the same engaging grin.

A last word on the people and the places where I 'sported and played' in my youth. Why, in a country where we have had no folk-hero since the days of Cuchulainn, was Christy Ring never made a freeman of the city of Cork?

A Teaching Life Begins

Anyone who walks along a corridor leading to the classroom where his first class are waiting for him does so with a certain amount of trepidation. I was probably fortunate in that I was initiated gradually into the teaching world. A temporary appointment in Mallow was followed by a year-long stay in Skibbereen.

The Christian Brothers had taught in Mallow until 1877 when they were ordered to leave by the parish priest, Father O'Regan, and despite the protests of the townspeople they did so.

The reason for their departure is rather confused but it does appear as if the determination of the Brothers not to affiliate to the Board of Education was central to the issue. Their intention not to do so meant that they and their school would then be dependent on the parish.

They were replaced by the Patrician Brothers and by the time of my arrival these had long been in residence in what is still known as the Academy. There was a great deal of goodwill towards them in the town, and the local landlord, Sir Jephson-Norreys of Mallow Castle, granted them the site on which the present school is built.

After my two months in Mallow, I went to Skibbereen where, by a strange coincidence, the new secondary school was the indirect result of a feud in another part of Ireland between the Church and a teaching Order of Brothers.

I had never travelled on the Skibbereen train until that autumn day when I set out to take up a position at St Fachtna's High School. I can, however, recall the bemused expression of the clerk at the Albert Quay station where I was enquiring about departure times, when an American tourist asked if it had a restaurant car!

The name 'Cork/Bandon and South Coast Railway' should

have warned him that it did not quite match what were probably his boyhood dreams of real locomotives thundering across limitless plains. All it did as it shuffled along on its west-bound journey was to cause cows to turn away and graze in some remote and less noisy corner of the field.

Nevertheless, it did seem conscious of its importance as it served no less than fifteen stations while affording an unrivalled means of seeing the countryside. Many a returning emigrant must have watched eagerly as the stations, with their raised platforms and wooden waiting-rooms, came into view: Waterfall, Ballinhassig, Crossbarry and Kinsale Junction, Upton, Bandon, Gaggin and Clonakilty Junction, Desert, Ballineen, Dunmanway, Knockbuidhe, Drimoleague, Aughaville, Madore.

The trains were often unpredictable in their behaviour, as much depended upon the quality of the coal and in 1938 supplies of coal from England and Wales were beginning to become scarce as the threat of a European war grew. The trains had scarcely left the city terminus than they paused before attacking the gentle slope which led to the Chetwynd Viaduct and the first stop at Waterfall. There they drew breath before crossing the high ground to Ballinhassig.

At each stop a station-master, resplendent in dark-blue livery, was happy to engage the engine-driver in conversation before reluctantly, or so it seemed, authorising the train to depart. Boxes of eggs, crates containing live poultry, sacks of fertiliser, bicycles, barrels of stout, fishing nets, filled the luggage van and often overflowed into the passenger compartments. No one heeded the regulation that would divide passengers into first-class, second-class and third-class men and women, nor was smoking frowned upon. Travel by rail was still a social occasion.

After its sixty-mile journey through meadowland and woodland, past lakes and streams, it pulled up, appropriately enough, almost beside the West Cork Hotel in Skibbereen.

That autumn of 1936 remains in my mind as one of long sunlit days. Each afternoon when school ended, I explored the marvellous coastline and the many sandy beaches, none more than ten miles distant from the town. Horse-drawn reapers and binders clacked about the small hilly fields. Beaches were deserted, the bungalows at Tragumna closed and shuttered, the last of the hay in the haggards.

Skibbereen was typical of Irish towns in the 'thirties. People lived at home, often in the house where they were born, and took their pleasure from the Annual Show, the hurling and football, the visiting circus, the whist drive followed by supper and dance (all for half a crown) and, if they had social pretensions, a tennis tournament at Lios Ard, the ancestral home of The O'Donovan, chief of the clan.

I found 'digs' in Bridge Street with Tess O'Brien. She had other lodgers, one of whom, Seán O'Driscoll, a teacher in the town, was the grandson of another Seán O'Driscoll, also a teacher, who had acted as chairman at the first meeting of the Phoenix Literary Society in Union Hall in 1863. When word of this was conveyed to the National Board of Education, O'Driscoll was dismissed and forced to emigrate.

St Fachtna's was run by the De La Salle Brothers. It had absorbed the much older 'University and Intermediate School' of which Mr Hogan was principal. Schools with such titles would appear to have succeeded the 'hedge schools', and many of them led a precarious existence until the written examination came to replace patronage as a means of entry to the British Civil Service as well as to the British army and navy. Then, when it seemed that they might have prospered and given the lay teacher an alternative to the emigrant ship, there came a wave of religious-inspired enthusiasm for teaching and the lay teacher was relegated to a subordinate if not a menial position.

Of the few lay schools that continued to exist, many were lay schools only in name. Mr Hogan's school was typical. In an advertisement he announced that 'This school is established under the Patronage of the Most Rev the Bishop and Clergy of the Diocese and supplies a high-class literary and professional education'.

The story of the coming of the De La Salle Brothers to Skibbereen had its background in a controversy which had gone on for almost eighty years in another part of Ireland. In December 1859 Mrs Julia Conmee, a well-to-do Catholic living in Roscommon, made her will. Under the terms of this will she requested that when all other legacies had been paid, the residue of her property should be handed over to the superior-general of the Institute of the Brothers of the Christian Schools in Ireland and his two assistants-general, as trustees for the establishment of a school for the education of poor male children.

The Christian Brothers were, it appeared, quite willing to

establish such a school but the provision, maintenance and staffing was at the time beyond their means. Letters passed between the bishop of the diocese (Elphin) and successive superior-generals of the Christian Brothers. From these letters it is clear that the real obstacle was the effect that another second-level school would be likely to have on the numbers in the diocesan seminary. The bishop chose to ignore the many resolutions passed by public bodies in the county asking that the Christian Brothers be introduced into the town.

That nothing was done for seventy years to make use of Mrs Conmee's bequest has to be attributed to episcopalian intransigence. In what he must have hoped would break the deadlock, the bishop had the parish priest of Roscommon town, Father Cummins,[1] write to the superior-general of the Christian Brothers informing him that 'the Bishop, as far as I know his mind, is willing to receive you provided, you undertake no Secondary teaching, but devote yourself to the programme of Technical Schools, or that of an Agricultural College'. These conditions, not altogether unexpectedly, the Christian Brothers found unacceptable.

In the summer of 1930 Brother Shanahan of the De La Salle Order went, on the invitation of the bishop, to Roscommon as principal of the National School, the headmaster of which had retired. Some of the townspeople, fearing that this might mean the end of their hopes of having the Christian Brothers, called a meeting to protest against what they considered to be a contravention of Mrs Conmee's intentions. The bishop saw this as a defiance of his authority and, in a letter read at all Masses on the Sunday morning of the meeting, announced: 'We are pained that a public meeting has been summoned with a view to discussing the school question which we, the Bishop of the Diocese, have already decided'.[2]

On the day of the public meeting, Monsignor Cummins, addressing the congregation at all the Masses, stated that he objected to being summoned to a meeting from the dead walls of the town and, in a direct reference to those responsible for calling the meeting, said, 'It was the act not of the old stock of Roscommon but of the ignorant rabble of the town, some of whom were only a few years in the parish and got very little

1. 2 September 1920.
2. 17 August 1930.

respect in the place they came from. If these Brothers (the Irish Christian Brothers) came into the parish they would probably starve and beggar the schools.... No matter what meetings were held, the Irish Christian Brothers would never come into the parish.'

The bishop made use of almost identical words in the course of a letter to the provincial, Brother Brendan O'Herlihy, of the De La Salle Order. His letter (17 August 1930), in which he rejected a proposal to have the De La Salle Brothers in the primary school and the Christian Brothers in the secondary, ended with the words 'but we will never agree to allow the Christian Brothers into Roscommon in any capacity'.

In an effort to have the matter decided once and for all, a Schools Committee which had been set up in the town determined to seek legal advice. This was done and the case of the Conmee Bequest came before Judge Johnston in the High Court in July 1931. The court asked that as a first step all monies in the hands of the trustees should be lodged in court. A scheme was then prepared for the use of these monies and a defence was entered by the ecclesiastical authorities.

Before a date for the hearing was fixed, the Catholic hierarchy, fearing unwelcome publicity, sent word through the Papal Nuncio that the parties concerned should withdraw the case from the civil courts and submit the issue to Rome. This was done and on 23 July 1936 the judges gave their verdict. In substance it said that the right of administering the legacy of Mrs Conmee belonged to the Irish Christian Brothers.

While the litigation was making its tedious way through the courts, the De La Salle Brothers were invited to open a secondary school in Skibbereen. In the course of a letter dated 25 January 1936, Bishop Casey of Ross wrote 'I have a sort of Secondary School here, taught by only one man, and consequently a failure. It used to be a good school in old times, with an efficient staff and could, I'm sure, be so again. I am writing to the Irish Christian Brothers, the Presentation Brothers and the Patrician Brothers, asking them to see the place and make an offer as to taking over the school. I am prepared to put the school itself in perfect repair, and to provide a site for a house. Beyond that I cannot bind myself. Perhaps the proposition may interest you. If you wish to see the place let me know'. By summer of the following year an agreement had been reached between the De La Salle Brothers and Bishop Casey. Almost at the same time i.e. July 1937, the Bishop of Elphin was writing to the Provincial of the De La Salle Order informing him that, consequent upon the decision of the Sacred Rota, his Brothers should be withdrawn from Roscommon. It was these brothers who formed the nucleus of the community who came to live at North Street, Skibbereen.

The first intimation the townspeople of Skibbereen had of their coming was when the bishop, speaking at the 12 o'clock Mass on the first Sunday in August, announced that he had invited them to take over the school where Mr Hogan — and later Mr Duggan — had for so long laboured.

I came to know Daniel Duggan well and can remember his telling me that he had been taught Latin, Greek and a little French by a 'spoiled priest' named Cadogan who lived near Skehanore on the road to Ballydehob. His school seems to have led a precarious existence and when Edward Ensor of the Board of Education arrived there on inspection in 1909, there were but twenty pupils.

Duggan, whose modest qualifications for schoolmastering showed him to have been a 2nd Arts student at the Royal University and a candidate for the BA degree, had taken over the school from Hogan in 1900. At that time he had no assistant and taught all subjects in one 'badly lighted' room. Ensor's report revealed the lack of what today would be considered certain essential amenities. Under the heading 'Description of Schoolhouse' is to be found the observation, 'Urinals: None, Lavatories: None'. Nor was any provision made for activities outside of the classroom. Under the heading 'Recreation', Ensor noted 'Games organised by staff: None; Compulsory Games: None; Drill: None; Provision of exercise on wet days: None'.

The academic standing of the school seems to have been in keeping with the unpretentious nature of the building. Of the two pupils taking Junior Grade French, one was said by the inspector to be a persistent truant who 'does not attend more than once a week and knows nothing'. Nor did the headmaster escape criticism. Ensor remarked that 'his articulation is extremely indistinct and it is hard to follow and understand him'.

Poor Mr Duggan. It cannot have been easy to teach school for almost forty years with never more than one other assistant and survive on the fees. Fees amounted to no more than a few shillings a term and as he never had many examination candidates, the

Results Fees payable on these by the Commissioners of Intermediate Education could not have enriched him. He was extremely sociable and enjoyed the company of the other teachers in the town where Austen Sweetman, principal of Abbeystrewery School, and Jer MacCarthy, principal of the Abbey School, were among his closest friends. He had a fine library of English and classical literature and treasured in particular a copy of *The Council Book of the Corporation of Youghal*. I remember that book as I have since seen it catalogued at a figure not far short of £1,000.

The events which led to the arrival of the De La Salle Brothers in the town were unusual. Not quite so dramatic were the circumstances of my own arrival. I was having a swim at the Lee Baths when someone shouted 'Help'. It came from a young lad who had got a sudden cramp in the water and, while he was in no danger, myself and another swimmer helped him to the bank.

After he had recovered from the shock, we got talking and he told me how his cousin had left a teaching post in Skibbereen to go to England and that he was taking this young lad with him that evening.

I had never heard of the school in Skibbereen though I knew that the De La Salle Order were long established some twenty miles from Cork, in Macroom. On impulse, I decided to send my CV to the Superior in Skibbereen.

I had a reply almost at once asking me to attend for interview at the Victoria Hotel on the following Saturday. I had never been in the Victoria Hotel where I found Brother Nilus and Brother Cyril finishing their lunch. What I remember most clearly of that interview is that the coffee they offered me tasted so differently from the Irel coffee at home and that the cups were so small.

Brother Nilus, the Superior of the school, was particularly eager that the teacher appointed should be able to offer drawing at least to Intermediate Certificate level, and here my year at the Crawford Municipal School of Art may well have turned the scales in my favour. Brother Cyril was glad to learn of my interest in Gaelic games, though for various reasons I was never asked to show my skills in either hurling or football — which was, perhaps, just as well.

Before we parted, I had been offered and had accepted the job vacated by Michael O'Shea who, with his cousin, was by then an exile in London.

My arrival in the town coincided with Glandore Regatta and

my landlady suggested that I should cycle over. She gave me clear directions, 'Go east the road past Shepperton Lakes until you come to Leap and then follow the road beside the sea.' When I reached Glandore I looked down from the sea-wall on a scene of enchantment: a landlocked harbour where dozens of pleasure boats, some four-oared rowing boats and a few small yachts swayed at anchor against a background of cream-washed houses and wooded hills.

The big event of the day was the race between the four-oared boat from Reengaroga and that from Myross and Glandore. Rivalry was intense between the two crews, each in a boat built by Skinner of Baltimore. I have no memory of the result but I do remember Bandon Pipers' Band marching down the slipway almost into the water to hail the winners.

Glandore Regatta was not an occasion for sun-bright parasols, summer frocks and striped blazers; nor was it an occasion when the oarsmen, for the most part seated happily on upturned barrels, seemed in any hurry to put to sea. When they did so, oars were fitted with difficulty into rowlocks and a critical eye might have detected a certain lack of unison in the subsequent rise and fall of the blades. Nobody cared and the evening shadows had begun to lengthen by the time the loudspeaker asked crews for the last race to go to the starting-point. It was a day out and the night was far advanced before the sounds of 'Skibbereen' and 'Bantry Bay' died away over the water.

A little over a week later I decided to avail of the last of the season's excursions to Ballydehob where the NACA were holding a sports meeting. I travelled there in a manner which may be unique in railway history. The excursion train, with an open observation car at the rear, left Skibbereen at midday. It was no more than a mile outside the town when it stopped and began to reverse. This caused some dismay among the passengers who found it hard to explain such odd behaviour on the part of the train. The answer was to be seen in a Pickwickian figure on the platform. 'Sonny' Goggin, director of the Skibbereen-Schull Tramway and Light Railway Company, had been forgotten!

The sportsfield was situated in a setting of great natural beauty. The Fastnet and Carbery's Hundred Isles lay to the south and the ruins of the O'Mahony castle of Rosbrin stood out on a nearby headland. All the prominent athletes were gathered in that small rock-circled field: Willie Nestor, Ned Tobin, Maurice

Curtin, Con O'Callaghan, Leslie Cuttriss, Jack Coveney, P.J. Aherne and the Guiney brothers from Kanturk — Jack, Paddy and Ted.

At the end of the day as the shadows lengthened and the sea wind freshened, the last event of the day was announced — the 56lb over the bar. An event demanding suppleness of wrist as well as strength, an event for men who knew what it was to feed the sheaves to a threshing-mill for the length of an autumn day. Florrie O'Mahony and Maurice Curtin had failed at sixteen feet. Danno Mahony, world wrestling champion, who was home on a holiday from the United States, was invited to have a try. Handing his jacket to an onlooker, he loosened his collar, glanced up and slung the weight high over the bar. It was a moment to set beside the triumph of Matt the Thresher in Knocknagow.

The sun set beyond the walls of the castle and the crowd moved slowly down the hillside, each with memories of an unforgettable day.

Skibbereen was a place where strange things happened. On that Sunday evening I was invited for a drink at a hotel convenient to the railway station. During the evening a loud knock, followed by the words 'Guards on duty', sent the customers scurrying to seek refuge as glasses were hurriedly emptied and lights turned off. One customer simply went into a bedroom where he was later found with his bowler hat and boots on in bed! Another ventured fully clothed into the river Ilen which flowed behind the hotel, preferring to run the risk, a very slight one, of drowning rather than face the shame of being found on a licensed premises on a Sunday. I lay hidden in a large linen basket, where I remained until the Guards put their notebooks away and went off to pursue the other evildoers of those distant days, the 'unlighted cyclists'.

One of those sheltering with me in that hotel basement was Eoin 'the Pope' O'Mahony who had been out at Rosbrin. There can never have been anyone quite like Eoin. While other boys of his age on the Douglas Road, where he lived with his parents at Dunmahon, may have expressed a wish to become engine-drivers, Eoin is believed to have made clear his ambition to be Pope — hence his pseudonym 'the Pope'. He could be said to have become instead a Citizen of the World. Whether hurrying, as I once met him in Oliver Plunkett Street, to send a telegram to Otto of Hapsburg on the occasion of the prince's birthday, or making his way, invariably on foot, to place a wreath on some forgotten patriot's grave or arranging a memorial service in Christ Church Cathedral and mass in the Chapel Royal of Dublin Castle for Chevalier Wogan Browne, a Jacobite soldier killed in 1754, Eoin seemed at all times to be everywhere.

St Fachtna's High School in Skibbereen was a cold, cheerless building both within and without. It was heated by electricity but it did seem that the heat in the classrooms was maintained only at a level which ensured that no pupil died of hypothermia. In the winter of that year, 1938-39, it must often have been a near thing.

The Bishop of Ross was a next-door neighbour and from the beginning showed a keen interest in the school. Rumours were even then beginning to circulate that he might well be the last bishop of a diocese whose historic boundaries were those of the O'Driscoll clan. Becoming part of the diocese of Cork had no appeal for a people whose ancestors had sent their bishop to represent them at the Council of Trent in the sixteenth century.

It did lose its independence in 1747 only to have it restored a century later. That was not the end of its vicissitudes and it was the intervention of Archbishop Croke of Cashel that saved it when in 1877 the bishops of Cork and Kerry cast covetous eyes on it. It lingered on until 1954 when, after eight hundred years during which for the most part it was a separate diocese, Ross became an appendage of the diocese of Cork.

An interesting feature of the amalgamation was that the then Bishop of Cork, Dr Lucey, was a stout opponent of centralising power. He had opposed the closing down of creameries, post offices and police barracks in rural areas and had intervened personally to prevent the amalgamation of national schools. The decision however rested with Rome and the eleven parishes of Ross came under his jurisdiction and despite spasmodic protests have remained part of the diocese of Cork. The eleven parishes are those which from medieval times have affirmed their fealty to Rome: Skibbereen, Castlehaven, Aughadown, Ardfield and Rathbarry, Barryroe, Kilmeen, Clonakilty and Darrara, Kilmacabea, Rath and the Islands, Lisavaird and Rosscarbery, Timoleague and Clogagh.

The other lay teacher was Danny O'Leary from Inchigeela who proved himself to be a tenacious footballer when he turned out with the local team. He was to give loyal service to the school where he continued to teach until his retirement in 1971.

When classes ended on a Saturday, the two of us often set off for Cork in his car, which may well have been the ancestor of all Ford Prefect cars. He was the only one who understood its mechanical eccentricities and was always ready with a can of boiling water before it could be persuaded to move even on a summer's day. En route it became so incontinent that we never dared set out without several cans of water. Some parts were missing altogether and one had a good view through gaps in the floorboards of the road whizzing past.

It also showed a marked dislike at being asked to go out on winter nights. Either the water froze in those pre-anti-freeze times, or the lights failed, forcing us to open (sic) the windscreen and focus the faint light of a torch on the road ahead.

At 'Norton', now the residence of the Brothers of the De La Salle Order, lived the best-known solicitor in the county, Jasper Travers Wolfe. He had a huge practice and was a recognised authority on conveyancing and problems relating to land. Naturally enough, he was not unfamiliar with the 'romantic' nature of the courtship rituals in an area of small farms and large families. Well-stocked farms were few and not all the land was in good heart. But even he must have been surprised when a client of his, a small farmer who had buried his first wife, came to announce his intention of re-marrying. The solicitor counselled prudence, warning of the possible difficulties involved in dividing land between the children of the first wife and also making provision for the second wife. The farmer listened patiently before blurting out, 'Sure, Mr Wolfe, for all they'd ate you wouldn't be without one'!

His reputation was not confined to this world if we are to believe informed gossip of the time. After the death of Charlie Kennedy of North Street, whom Jasper had briefed on many occasions, it appeared that St Peter was in a quandary.

Charlie had led an exemplary life and seemed well qualified for entry through the Golden Gates. He had, however, on one occasion defended the owner of a greyhound whose colouring changed dramatically during a shower of rain. The case for the prosecution was that the dog had been substituted and St Peter was not entirely happy with the defence put forward. He therefore decided to consult the supreme legal authority known to the celestial powers — Jasper Wolfe.

And so it came about that Jasper was called to his eternal reward shortly after that of his friend, Charlie Kennedy.

My departure from St Fachtna's at the end of the school year was prompted more by a desire to take up a position at Lota on the outskirts of Cork city than by any dissatisfaction with life in Skibbereen. It was then, and probably still is, a marvellously gregarious place. No one ever alighted from a train there unnoticed, no one was ever born or died there unrecorded. It is a friendly, talkative town with no need of a town crier or gossip columist.

Nor is it all that difficult to conduct a conversation across the street even if traffic does at times cause an unwelcome interruption. Most of the talk has an extravagant boastfulness and P.J. O'Sullivan, a well-known figure in the town in the 'thirties, challenged a Clonakilty rival to a score of bowls in order to prove that he, O'Sullivan, was 'the greatest man of this or any generation'. O'Sullivan is credited with having walked the ten miles to Ballydehob in one hour and twenty minutes, which was slightly faster than the train.

In many ways life in Skibbereen was a microcosm of life as lived in many Irish country towns. Surface gaiety but a certain unrest, even turbulence, beneath. A smouldering awareness of some inner energy which finds expression often on issues which an outsider finds difficult to understand; the appointment of a teacher, doctor, postmistress, the siting of a creamery, the erection of a monument.

In Skibbereen there is also an ethnic richness which is not to be found elsewhere, a pluralism not only of stock but of religious sects. Where else in Ireland, within the confines of a few parishes, will you come upon such a variety of names as Caverley, Camier, Dukelow, Trinder, Chudleigh, Swanton and Salter? Edith Somerville may have got it right when, in a letter dated 1894 to her cousin Martin Ross, she wrote, 'I see that one day the Skibbereen district will be a fifth province of Ireland — refusing to receive Home Rule, and governed by Aylmer, (Master of the West Carbery Hunt) under a special warrant from the Queen'.

A School with a Difference

No inspectors, no syllabus, no curriculum, no timetable, no textbooks, no homework! A teacher's dream come true. For the realisation of such a dream, I had to thank Hitler and the Second World War.

It happened that in 1939, soon after the outbreak of war, the Brothers of Charity in Chorley, Lancashire, were notified that the area in which their novitiate was situated was a possible danger-zone. They decided to seek temporary refuge in Ireland and bought Lota House near Glanmire, county Cork.

Lota had passed through many hands in the course of centuries. In the fourteenth century the Galway family lived on the land fronting the estuary of the Lee, where today the roads to Dublin and to Waterford divide. Their estates were confiscated after the defeat of James II and the family fled to France.

The new owners were the Rogers, merchants of considerable standing in the city. For close on two hundred years their connection with Lota continued, until in 1854 it passed into the hands of the Wood family. Although the interior is much altered, the house is substantially that which Arthur Young looked upon in 1776 when, in his *Tour of Ireland*, he gave his impressions of its setting: 'On the north side of the river which is much better planted, particularly at Lota, the ground rises in bold ascents, adorned with many beautifully situated country houses. The view of Lota is charming, a fine lawn rising from the waters, with noble spreading woods reaching on each side, the house has a pleasant front, with lawns shooting into the woods'.

One of the changes made at Lotà between the time of Young's visit to Cork and the coming of the Brothers was the placing in the Venetian window at the head of the great double ramp staircase of the armorial bearing of the Crowley family, the last private owners of the house.

Having purchased the house, the Brothers advertised for a teacher of the novices. I applied and was asked to call. No one could say that I was interviewed. When Brother Godric walked across the gravel to meet me, proffering the snuff of which he was very fond, I sensed that I had been appointed. Godric was circular in shape, jolly in manner and, as I was to discover, inexhaustible in doing good.

That was the late August of 1939 and during the year that followed I was the sole teacher of fourteen young men ranging in age from fifteen to eighteen. I was a sort of headmaster without portfolio, exercising an authority that Keate of Eton or Arnold of Rugby might have envied. And unlike them, I had no interfering governors and no importunate parents to trouble my days. The Brother Superior was fully occupied in laying the foundations of what has since become a residential hospital and school for moderately and severely handicapped children.

The two who stand out in my mind as having worked tirelessly for the Home in those early days were Brother Godric and Mrs Alice Nalder. When Brother Godric sought your help, there was little point in seeking escape by pleading real or imaginary commitments, whereas immediate assent to his requests made you feel that you shared in the goodness which radiated from him.

Were Nobel Prizes awarded to persons who in winter brave the winds that come howling up the Lee estuary straight from Siberia, Alice Nalder must surely have had a claim. Each morning she cycled from her home at Ashton on the Blackrock Road, calling en route at the Baltimore Stores in MacCurtain Street for fish-heads, etc. with which to make soup for the inmates. She had learned much from the experiments carried out by Sir Michael Abercrombie in Scotland and knew how much a well-balanced diet contributed to the well-being of the disturbed and disabled. Having no children of their own, both she and her husband helped to love and care for those in Lota.

On my first meeting with my students, we decided against having any textbooks and also that we would arrange in advance what subject was to be studied each day. Thus, we might decide to devote a whole day to Latin or divide the day in two and study

English in the morning and History in the afternoon. We did occasionally move from the study of purely secular subjects to devote a few hours to Religious Education. Here I felt less at ease believing that God, if he takes an interest in the various interpretations of his teaching, might have had reason to be dissatisfied with me.

The work of the Brothers, who devote their lives to the less fortunate, gives to such places as Lota an air of remoteness from reality, but there is nothing unreal in the dedication which they show towards those unable, in many cases, to do anything for themselves. They radiate cheerfulness, they make light of the most unpleasant tasks, they work unbelievably long hours, their patience seems inexhaustible. There is no need to go on. Lota is a place where life is made use of to count the gifts that life distributes in ways which can never seem fair to our limited intelligence.

The class was quite sharply divided on the issue of Christ's attitude to the money-changers in the Temple whom they saw as twentieth-century entrepreneurs. And they were almost all critical of bringing back Lazarus from the dead. This they thought was in very bad taste and, indeed, when in later life I saw him as shown in Scorsese's 'The Last Temptation of Christ', I agreed wholeheartedly with them.

When the sun shone, we emerged on the terrace fronting the house and went through a series of movements which would have shamed geriatrics. This we referred to as Physical Education! There was an embarrassing moment for me when a newly-professed brother, who had been a drill instructor in the British Army, arrived. He spoke to the students of the need for fitness and stressed the importance of their biceps, triceps and many other muscles which had lain happily dormant during my gymnastic lessons.

On summer days we walked down the front drive, crossed the main Cork/Waterford road and entered the grounds of Inchera where we had permission to swim. This had once been known as Gray's Island but after the death of Colonel Gray who was killed at the battle of Knocknanos, the property was sold and later passed into the hands of the Murphy family, the Cork firm of brewers. Mr Charles Murphy, the Managing Director of the company, invited us all for a picnic on the lawn in front of his house at the end of that school year.

I enjoyed those mornings cycling down to Lota, especially as there was no great emphasis by me, the teacher, on strict punctuality. The road seemed to have changed but little over the years. Lover's Walk, which meets the main road opposite the old Tivoli railway station, was once Leper's Lane, and rising above it are the hills which reminded Micheál MacLiammoir of 'tea cosies embroidered with flowers'.

Sheltering within one of these 'tea cosies' was Woodlands, once the house of Sir John Arnott, one of the consortium of Cork businessmen who bought the Gresham Hotel in Dublin. Farther down the road was O'Callaghan's Gate with its remarkable stone carving of a dog over the main entrance. This was erected in memory of a dog who, on seeing his master drowning in the muddy waters of the estuary, swam out and helped him ashore. The man survived but the dog fell dead.

I had a number of 'markers' by which to gauge the time. As I passed the Oriental Bar across the road from 'the Fisheries', the four-oared boats would be preparing to set out for a day's fishing on Lough Mahon and 'Micka' Brennan of Sarsfields would wave as he cycled up from Riverstown to his work at Dunlop's.

That year in Lota was one of unalloyed joy. With the spectre of examinations banished, learning became a shared activity. The well-stocked library was our greatest resource and this we really 'plundered' for its treasures. What it yielded was not measurable but I like to think that it was of enduring value.

The idea of a school with a flexible timetable in which teachers and pupils shared control, with subjects taught by a variety of people not necessarily graduates but interested in the individual subject, was first outlined to me by the Swiss-born author and teacher, Anthony Kerr.

Anthony Kerr deserved a biography and he may well have got one by now as I lost track of him. I think that I can safely say that no author ever approached the writing of a serious book, such as his *Schools of Europe* and *Universities of Europe*, in quite the same way as he did. He simply got on his motorbike when the school in Edinburgh in which he taught closed for holidays and motorcycled all over Europe.

During a divorce action brought by his wife, he was asked why he was so often absent from the home where his wife and children were living, and he gave a disarmingly frank reply. He said that compiling the information on which his books were based required him to travel widely and frequently.

For all the speed with which they were written, the books remain valuable records of the systems he examined. He never sought to pass judgement but presented information clearly and concisely, and drew from it his own conclusions. He was ahead of most educational thinking of the time when he recommended that all teachers should, when in mid-career, be given a career break.

My own 'career break' came rather early. In 1943 to be exact. In the winter of that year I might have been seen walking down Patrick Street in uniform. Not, as one might reasonably have surmised, as a member of the armed forces who had enlisted for the duration of the war but as a traffic officer in Aer Lingus.

The title was a shade misleading. In those days the duties of a traffic officer consisted of issuing tickets, checking the weight of passengers and baggage and being generally knowledgeable on air travel between Collinstown, later to become known as Dublin Airport, and Liverpool or Manchester.

We were as well as I can remember seven: Geraghty, Mellerick, Mayne, Breathnach, Byrne, MacBrien and myself. We were based at 44 Upper O'Connell Street, Dublin. There was but one airport to which we could send passengers — Speke Airport near Liverpool. There was but one fare: single, £4, and return £7 4s.

The big event of the week was the arrival every Tuesday of four cattle-buyers from England who came for the Wednesday market at the North Circular Road. Their plane was usually piloted by Captain Greenhalgh, Captain Hammond or Captain Kennedy. When the cattle men returned to the office on Wednesday afternoon, they were laden with parcels of meat from Moore Street. Once they had their tickets checked, they usually took a four-wheel horse cab to Binn's Bridge, Drumcondra, there to await in a hostelry known to them the coming of the bus for the airport.

That the company prospered may be due in no small measure to the early departure of many who, like myself, were singularly ill-suited to the quickly growing world of air travel. What may have hastened my own departure was 'the Monteagle affair'. I was alone in the office when Lord Monteagle, a director of the Irish Tourist Association, arrived one day to book a seat to Speke Airport. There were no other passengers that day and as he had but one suitcase, I did not need to have it weighed. However, I did so and as it exceeded the limit allowed, I charged him the excess baggage rate, though he could have taken the equivalent of a suite of furniture on the lightly-laden plane.

To compound that blunder, I failed to reserve a room at the Adelphi Hotel in Liverpool, as he had requested. In the event, he arrived during the black-out to be told that there was no room available as there was no reservation in his name. There is no record of his feelings when later he found that I had issued him a three-monthly ticket when he was returning within three days!

While usually there were two or three of us in the office to deal with customer enquiries, it happened that I was again the only one 'on duty', if that is not a misuse of the phrase, when a woman came in to purchase a ticket for herself and her dog. Difficult as I found it to issue a ticket for a human being, the 'ticketing' of a dog was altogether too much for me. I told her that while of course it would be a pleasure for the company to carry the dog, it would first have to spend twelve months in quarantine.

As the war clouds lifted, the company decided to advertise a combined air and rail ticket to certain destinations in Great Britain. This initiative did not appeal to me. I found it difficult enough to issue a ticket to Speke Airport without compounding the problem by attempting to convey the passenger any farther. So, in the interests of the customer and of my own sanity, I did nothing to publicise that venture.

We took it in turn to open the office at 8.30 each morning. O'Connell Street was then marvellously quiet — a few trams lumbering along to and from Nelson's Pillar, the swish of bicycles and the clip-clop of horse-drawn vans and cabs. The first task was to ensure that the office cat had left no mouse in the path of any customer and to water the lone plant that always seemed about to blossom but never did.

A large globe stood on the counter, possibly to signify the opportunities of air travel to the uttermost ends of the earth. My innermost prayer was that no customer would be so daft as to wish to go there while I was on duty.

In that summer of 1944 hopes of an end to the war were raised when the German Army seemed to be on the retreat. Aer Lingus began to formulate plans for expansion, necessitating the recruitment of more staff. Promotional opportunities within the company increased almost overnight.

Those of us in the O'Connell Street office were summoned

'upstairs' to where the General Manager, Gerry Dempsey, the chief accountant, Mr Ingram and the office manager, Mr O'Riordan, formed an interviewing panel. I remember little of the questions put to me though I do recall the barely-suppressed smiles at my reply when asked about the engine-power of the Dakota planes which the company was then purchasing — 'four Royce-Whitney, 11,000 h.p. engines'!

That interview may have raised doubts in their minds about my role, if any, in their plans for the future. These doubts may have been strengthened when for some reason I found myself dealing with a customer. These duties I usually managed to leave to others. In this case, having sold a return ticket to Speke Airport (£7 4s), I found that I had only £2 16s in my 'float' at the end of the day. He had tendered a £10 note and I had given him back the cost of his ticket!

When, as was bound to happen, Aer Lingus looked round for some place where I might do least damage to the company's image, it was decided to send me to Rineanna. That was in the autumn of 1944 and Shannon Airport as such did not come into existence until a year later.

Mellerick, Breathnach and myself were comfortably lodged in a Moracrete bungalow and each evening we phoned the Garda barracks at Foynes to know if there were any 'operations' i.e. flying-boat arrivals, on the following day. On receipt of the news that there were none, and I never saw a flying-boat, we ordered breakfast in bed and only rose to help a neighbouring farmer named O'Dea with the hay.

With the hay saved and swallows beginning to gather in the evening sky for their southwards journey, I resigned. To his credit, Michael Twomey, the Station Manager, managed to express regret when I informed him of my decision.

To resign from service which, even in the early 'forties, held promise of promotion and adventure, may appear to have been folly. In my case, I shed the dark blue uniform with the bright buttons without regret, The air was an element for which I was not suited.

When in the autumn I closed the classroom door and turned to face a class of new faces, it was with a feeling of total satisfaction. The 'sheltered workshop' atmosphere of the classroom suited me. Once within its walls, I felt sheltered from the shocks which face other professional groups. It is an *aut vitam*, *aut culpam* situation where, if the teacher commits no gross misdemeanour, he may move along a well-defined path to retirement. I had found that it suited me.

Any interest that I might have been expected to show in matters political developed somewhat late in my life. In the 1940s a nationwide teachers' strike, together with the imprisonment, often without trial, of suspects had created a climate of dissatisfaction with the government.

A new party was formed called *Clann na Poblachta*. It met with a good deal of optimistic enthusiasm throughout the country though Cork remained rather unmoved. However, after a visit by Noel Hartnett and Sean MacBride, a branch was formed in the city. I went along to a meeting in the home of Roibeard Breathnach, a lecturer in Irish at UCC, which Seamus Murphy, the sculptor, attended. Many of those whom I met there that evening were known to me from my earlier association with Ailtirí na hAiséirighe.

It was difficult to preach political revolution in a city where there was no yawning gulf between the rich and the poor and where the products that came in from the surrounding countryside were being distributed at least tolerably well.

There never was any militant trade unionism in Cork. Workers in the factories never lost a sturdiness of viewpoint which made them neither subservient nor class-embittered. With memories of the Civil War slow to die, the citizens remained politically rather than economically motivated.

Speakers for public meetings were difficult to get and I volunteered. It was a mistake. On the way to a meeting in a country town, each speaker was instructed to base his or her speech on some aspect of the Clann's policy document. On the way to a meeting in Athy Town Hall, Mac O'Rahilly gave me what I may call 'the Economic portfolio'! Thus it was for me to explain the following splendidly confident plan: 'A national monetary authority will be established, whose function will be to create currency and credit for the economic needs of full employment, and full production, and to provide credits, free of interest, for full employment and national development'.

Feeling rather as Roosevelt may have felt when he launched the New Deal, I mentioned blithely that our initial aim would be to repatriate our sterling assets. A cold voice from the hall interrupted me. 'How does Mr McElligott propose to do this?'

With some difficulty I suppressed an insane impulse to suggest sending over a rowing boat. I mumbled some incoherent phrases before the Chairman rescued me by asking if there were any other questions.

My career as a politician, as a public speaker and as an economist ended on that night in that quiet country town beside the river Barrow.

On but one occasion in my years of teaching did I take up a permanent position in my native city, and it was not a happy one. I was glad to obtain work near home and also to be in a school founded and controlled by a lay person. T.P. Leahy, the headmaster, was a Socialist politician *manqué*. From his days at University College, Cork, until he opened his own school at Camden Place, he cherished the dream of giving less well-off children the opportunity of a fuller education.

To open a lay school was to run the risk of clerical displeasure no less marked in Cork than elsewhere. To open a co-educational lay school was tantamount to an act of defiance. Leahy, a devout Catholic, told me that he had consulted ecclesiastical authorities before doing so. Their assent did not necessarily mean approval and many parents frowned on the idea of such a school when there were orders of nuns and monks well fitted to undertake the education of their children.

I had known Leahy at university where he was recognised as one of the most able students with a special interest in Irish. He had won the Ó Longáin Irish literary prize which, incidentally, was won in successive years by Sean O'Faolain and by Eileen Gould who later became his wife.

Very regrettably, by September 1946 when I joined his staff, his sight, which had never been good, had entirely failed. He strove with great courage not to allow the disability to affect the working of the school. He would on occasion take the seven flights of stairs leading to the top classroom two at a time and, given a problem in Advanced Calculus, I have seen him dictate each step leading to the solution while looking with sightless eyes towards where the river Lee flowed onward to the sea.

Teaching boys and girls in the same class was for me a new experience. There was much to enjoy. One day my classroom door flew open and an excited Betty O'Driscoll, entirely ignoring my presence, called to a girl at the back of the room, 'He's waiting for you below at the door.'

Assuming my best professional manner, I addressed Betty: 'Are you not aware, Betty, that it is one of the elementary rules of good manners that one must never enter a room, particularly a room in which someone older is engaged in the instillation of knowledge, without at first knocking?'

Betty looked at me for a moment as if to assure herself that I was real. Then turning to the class she said 'Wouldn't you feel for him!'

The first few months went by pleasantly and I was able to help outside of school hours by taking games, usually hurling on a pitch beside the Sacred Heart College on the Western Road. He also had me organise debates in which he took part and which we both enjoyed, but it was in the classroom that I resented his interference. He could not resist telling a teacher how a subject should be taught.

In my own case, he believed that all teaching in Irish should be oral and he had a blackboard removed from my room. I resented this, but in retrospect I am inclined to think that he was right. Undue emphasis on composition and grammar had done harm to the language revival.

I know that he in turn, resented my comments on the condition of the rooms and the lack, even, of desks in some of them. The building was in fact quite unsuitable as a school, being a four-storey house in bad repair beside a busy thoroughfare. On wet days, of which Cork has its share, rain came through the roof and large basins were provided for the classrooms on the top floor.

By the spring of 1947 Leahy and myself were scarcely on speaking terms and in March of that year I was given a week's notice. Had I got even a month's notice, I might have done nothing. As it was, I consulted a solicitor, William Hutch-Ryan.

The irony of the situation was that I had been inveighing against the summary dismissal of teachers by religious teaching orders. And I was now taking the first steps to bring a lay headmaster to court. My case rested on the right of a registered teacher to three months' notice. In addition, as my barrister Simon Kepple was to point out, Leahy was also obliged to make good any loss of incremental salary, if wrongful dismissal could be proved.

The case came before Judge Conroy in the Circuit Court. When, under cross-examination by Leahy's counsel, Stephen Barrett, I admitted having called a pupil a donkey, the Judge observed that if that was an offence, then he had been seriously slandered during his schooldays at Clongowes.

The court decided in my favour and the judge gave a decree for the full amount claimed, in addition to costs. The decision was appealed but when the High Court sat, counsel for the defendant said that he had received no instructions and agreed that the case be struck out.

So Leahy and I parted company but remained on good terms. Some twenty years later I met him at the famous 'Teach-In' at University College, Cork when he spoke trenchantly to a paper by Dr T.K. Whitaker on the economic problems of the State. Afterwards, we had a most friendly chat, all past animosities forgotten. He had come to interest himself in local politics, had been elected Lord Mayor and had married. Given his disability, he had achieved a great deal. Yet what mattered most to him, 'Leahy's College', scarcely outlived his death.

During periods of unemployment such as that following my dismissal by Leahy, my references had to be kept up-to-date. I was reluctant to alter my age, though I was reminded to do so at least once a year by Miss Barrett and Miss O'Shaughnessy, who did secretarial work for the Tip-Tap Typing Company in Cook Street and typed many CV's for me.

The reason behind my apparent indifference to the passage of time was, I consider, sound. I believed then and I still do that school principals favour neither the very young nor the very old. So it was that for a number of years I remained for academic purposes an unchanging thirty.

Nor was I inclined to limit the range of subjects which I offered to those on my degree. Happily, the day of the specialist subject teacher had not yet arrived and I don't think that I ever hesitated to apply for a position because of my unfamiliarity with a subject.

French I offered on the strength of having attended the Christmas party at the Berlitz School in Dublin. Art I offered with more confidence as there has always been a lack of unanimity even among experts in the field as to what constitutes Art. Commerce I found dishearteningly difficult and my inability to distinguish between Cash Book and Ledger a handicap. Religious Education posed no problem even though I could work up no great enthusiasm for the course in Apologetics and I do think th; Father Forde, the Diocesan Examiner, had grave reservatic about the orthodoxy of my opinions.

References were tricky things to deal with. First of all, many of my professors at UCC found me lacking in any of the qualities they could enthuse over. This was to be expected in view of my academic record and one professor contented himself with the bleak statement 'Mr McElligott was a student in my Department during the years 1931 to 1935 '. Not, it will be agreed, a remark calculated to catch the eye of a prospective employer.

Granted that it was succinct and unlikely to mislead, I still felt that it needed elaboration. A headmaster, on receipt of my application accompanied by such a reference, might be pardoned for not realising that the professor, lacking a good prose style, had contented himself with that one sentence. So, I set out to rectify the matter.

I did so in a manner of which I am proud. The 'reconstructed' reference was instrumental in having headmasters vying with one another in their eagerness to appoint me. And, lest they were ever tempted to seek confirmation of my many virtues from the professor, he died at a comparatively early age!

My teaching of Mathematics may have, indeed must, have aroused doubt in the mind of any headmaster with his ear to the keyhole of my classroom door. First of all, I have always disliked odd numbers. I look upon such digits as 3, 5, 7, and 9 as a mean conniving lot and far prefer the rotundity of the 2, 4, 6, 8 group.

When I set my class a problem, I made sure in advance that it involved these fat, contented digits and I felt that it was no accident that there were 2,240 lbs in a ton. Whenever I thought of that, I envisaged a line of little bags each weighing one lb and all adding up to the magnificence of a ton.

For the purpose of dealing with the classroom menace who insists on asking questions, I had furnished myself with a key to the mathematical textbooks of Hall & Stevens and Hall & Knight. To acquire these indispensable adjuncts to trouble-free teaching, I had to guarantee that such knowledge as the keys contained was for my personal use, provide character references and present evidence that I had no criminal record.

What brought about my undoing was the shift to the metric system. No longer were oz, pecks, bushels, and quarters of any use, no longer did roods, perches and furlongs together with pints, quarters and gallons provide material for mathematical problems. I had become obsolete.

I have no wish to recall such of my classes as were entered on the official records under 'Science: 1st Year B; Time,10a.m. to 10.45 a.m.; Teacher, McElligott.' True to my theory, which I hope someday to formulate as a pedagogical principle, that the true teacher teaches without regard for subject, I accepted a position as teacher of Chemistry to Junior classes.

My classroom must at times have resembled a Fire Station on 'Crisis Alert'. After my first week it was thought prudent to have buckets of water, sand and fire-extinguishers at the door of the laboratory whenever I was conducting experiments. These were not always successful but your true scientist is not deterred by failure. The headmaster apparently thought otherwise and found himself compelled at the end of the school-year to alter his staffing arrangements.

He did say, without, however, any great show of regret that this would mean parting company but that he would follow my future career with interest, but from a distance!

Leavetaking

There is little doubt that the satisfactions of life gain in intensity with advancing years. Speed seems to matter less. Time seems to matter more. So when you return to Cork, go by train rather than by road. You will then savour more intensely the gradual recall of familiar landmarks, as the train, having climbed up from Mallow, begins the run down from the heights above Rathduff.

Leaving Waterloo and Blarney on the right, the train affords a glimpse of the Eight-Arch bridge just as the hills above Shandon come into view. Below lies the city that was once no more than a cluster of huts beneath the great rock of Gillabbey.

For those of us born there, Cork is a catalogue of street and lane and alley with their associations that time has failed to erode. To walk among old houses, battered and weathered, is to come close to your origins, to be sharply aware of the past.

And you don't have to be born there to sense the atmosphere of seduction that hangs around every corner. When General Sir Carton de Wiert, after a lifetime spent travelling the world, was asked why he chose to live in Cork, he instanced the story of the little girl whom he met on his first visit to the city. When he asked her for directions as to where a road led, she replied 'Oh, that road will take you to any place you like'. Captivated by the reply, he bought Aghinagh House at Killenardrish and lived there until his death in 1963.

Cork people have never sought to conceal their zest for life. It shows itself in the unrestrained, almost explosive, outbursts of joy with which those who bring glory to their birthplace are greeted on their return. Few of those at school in the 'North Mon' in the 1930's are likely to forget the welcome to the victorious teams that won four Harty Cup finals in a row. Tar barrels blazed from Blackpool Bridge to Shandon Street where Mollie Owens ruled over all!

It is at such moments that some Gallic quality comes to the surface and kindles the enthusiasm of the entire city. In a lifetime spanning three-quarters of a century, it has never failed to delight me and I feel that it never will.

Certain human qualities are, I believe, communicable and it is this which I feel when, after an absence of years, I walk down Patrick Street and meet familiar faces. In fact, I still find myself wondering, when noticing unfamiliar faces, how they got there! For in Cork it is the unfamiliar that is remarkable.

From its earliest foundation, Cork was the right kind of stage-set for the theme and proportions of the drama that is its history. The hills surrounding it form a sort of proscenium arch and from each street and lane and square some spire or steeple may be seen.

The setting has changed but little. The course of the Lee valley may still be seen from Gurranebraher and the waters of Lough Mahon from the top of 'the Forty Steps'. With this changeless setting goes a certain reluctance to change in the people. What some see as torpor and sterility, I see as a reassuring sameness. The Coal Quay is still readily identifiable even if it has long been Cornmarket Street, the North Gate Bridge has yet to surrender its name and become Griffith Bridge and if Shandon still strikes the hours with less than rigorous punctuality, the citizens accept a certain eccentricity from such an old and venerable Protestant institution.

'Changelessness' is not to the liking of everyone. Writers like O'Connor and O'Faolain were sharply aware of the stifling constraints and the sense of stagnation that comes from living in a closed room. The 'closed room' may still exist but if it does, it has given to the city a social and communal cohesion which unites those born within it.

Such unity does not inhibit the capacity to develop rich diversities of personality. In an unstratified society such as Cork offers, the variations were almost limitless. In my own case, while the existence of wide variations was recognised, the chief drive was the striving for respectability. I can still feel the shame that I felt during periods of unemployment. I came to know all the back streets and lanes where I hoped to pass unnoticed on my way to Sunday mass or to the library in Tuckey Street.

All experience deepens feeling for place and people and I am ever aware of the good fortune that brought my parents to Cork and brought me into the world all those years ago.

Programme: Danno Mahony at the Cork Opera House, 1936